EDWARD THOMAS

A Critical Study

EDWARD THOMAS at Broughton Gifford,
from a photograph lent by Ann (Myfanwy) Thomas.

Edward Thomas

A Critical Study

H. COOMBES

BARNES & NOBLE
BOOKS
10 East 53d St., New York 10022
(a division of Harper & Row Publishers, Inc.)

Published in Great Britain by
Chatto & Windus

★

Published in the U.S.A. 1973 by:
HARPER & ROW PUBLISHERS, INC.
BARNES & NOBLE IMPORT DIVISION

★

Published in Canada by
Clarke, Irwin & Co. Ltd.

ISBN 06-491272-8

Printed in Great Britain

TO J. M. A.

Acknowledgments

MY THANKS are due to the following for their kind permission to use excerpts from the works named: A. & C. Black Ltd., *Beautiful Wales;* Jonathan Cape Ltd., *A Literary Pilgrim in England,* and *The Last Sheaf;* Chapman & Hall Ltd., *George Borrow,* and *The Life of the Duke of Marlborough;* Constable & Co. Ltd., *The Icknield Way;* J. M. Dent & Sons, Ltd., *The Heart of England, Oxford,* and *The South Country;* Gerald Duckworth & Co. Ltd., *Horae Solitariae, Rest and Unrest, Light and Twilight, The Happy-Go-Lucky Morgans,* and *Cloud Castle;* Faber & Faber Ltd., *Collected Poems* (of Edward Thomas), and *Selected Essays* by T. S. Eliot; Hutchinson and Co. Ltd., *Richard Jefferies;* Mrs Frieda Lawrence and W. Heinemann Ltd., various works of D. H. Lawrence; Mrs. Q. D. Leavis, an article on Richard Jefferies in *Scrutiny* (March 1938); Methuen & Co. Ltd., *Maurice Maeterlinck;* Thomas Nelson & Sons Ltd., *Keats;* Martin Secker & Warburg Ltd., *Algernon Charles Swinburne, Feminine Influence on the Poets,* and *Walter Pater.* Part of the chapter entitled 'The Poetry' has appeared in *Essays in Criticism,* and my thanks are due to the Editor, Mr F. W. Bateson, for permission to use it here.

Mr J. W. Haines talked to me more than once about his memories of Edward Thomas. And especially am I grateful to Mrs Helen Thomas for her personal kindness, for her readiness to give any information that might be helpful, and for her permission to use anything I wished from many books and letters.

H. C.

CONTENTS

' . . . It's a pleasant thing to hold an enemy in one's grasp, and as soon as I am rested I will place you in the path, and the light you boast of will guide my boot so that I can trample you to death.'

When she heard this sentence pronounced upon her, the glow-worm remained pensive for a while, but even then she did not lose heart nor did she despair of escaping, though she remained in the farmer's hand.

'Have you never thought, Squire Told,' she began gently, 'that, even if we exempt virtue and goodness, there are in the world other pleasant things more delightful than a mere possession of goods? Is there not the exquisite joy that beauty yields to its votaries, for who would wish his thought, upon such a night as this, to be occupied with the price of pork, with the manuring of a turnip field, or the killing of a little worm? How much better to contemplate the divine loveliness of the summer stars! Look upward and behold the glittering heavens! Does not such a sight awake in your mind a state of blessedness? Notice, too, I pray you, that heavy mass of blackness that is Madder Hill; see how it is set against the midnight sky. Does not the profound darkness of the hill suit the mild and deep melancholy that can join the Creator to the creature in one large sorrow? Hark you, listen to that distant sound, that heavy fall of the sea upon the summer beach! Think of the cool shining of the pebbles and the white loneliness of the great cliffs. Consider the eternal, the everlasting look of the sea itself. Think again, Mr. Told, for a moment, upon a white daytime flower. You should know all love and sorrow when you see a meek daisy—a small plant, but one that can exceed Solomon in all his glory.'

T. F. POWYS, *John Told and the Worm*

CHAPTER ONE

Life, Legend, and Repute

NORMALLY, legends are quick to gather around poets of any note, especially when they have died on the battlefield, and one would have thought that a man of whom one of the most widely read poets of our century, Mr Walter de la Mare, wrote in the 1930s that 'it is little less than tragic to think how comparatively unheeded in any public sense was his coming and going', and of whom a great literary critic, Dr. F. R. Leavis, wrote in the same decade, 'He was a very original poet who devoted great technical subtlety to the expression of a distinctively modern sensibility', would not lack by now at least that kind of fame. But the reader might justly wonder about the extent of fame those references have brought to Thomas, and might very well, despite a preface by Lloyd George here, an incidental remark there—as that of Lawrence of Arabia in a letter to Edward Garnett (1927): 'He must have been a beautiful person'—be prompted by the heading of this initial chapter to ask if there is in fact any Edward Thomas legend. Certainly neither his life nor his character was anything like Rupert Brooke's: his poetry has never been read in St Paul's Cathedral. Yet Helen Thomas's two books, *As It Was* and *World Without End*, have been and are, I would say, comparatively popular (and probably more widely read than his poetry), and together with the kind of attention he has mostly received in other places, they have produced a 'general impression' that is briefly this:

Edward Thomas is the author of some charming poems

about the English countryside; he loved the natural and familiar and homely things of England. His love of Helen and his married life were marked both by an intense bliss and an intense, strange sadness, the sadness (which underlay his whole life, or all but the whole) being an inevitable effect of his Celtic temperament. After having done a large amount of uncongenial hack-writing to keep off poverty, he discovered himself in poetry, and having enlisted in the army he overcame his 'demon' of melancholy and his self-doubts and died the death of a soldier-poet.

Such is, I believe, the substance of what legend there is. It is not in any sense a popular legend; and it is compounded of truth, misrepresentation, and the distortion that comes inevitably of simplifying. Possibly it is better that there should be an inadequate legend than none at all, but when the inadequacy or the deviations tend to put up a barrier against the full and balanced recognition of the *writer*, one of our aims must be to attempt to adjust with a redistribution of emphasis and a demonstration of the shortcomings or falsities.

Thomas is one of the few poets of our century whom we can go back to again and again. He gives plentifully to nature lovers, but he is more than a 'nature poet'. He has had, of course, some worthy spokesmen; but a perusal of the sum (or almost) of what has been written about him is likely to lead to the opinion that no poet of the century, with the exception of Isaac Rosenberg, has been so unjustifiably neglected. It seems clear that Thomas would not have done work of the quality that Rosenberg (who also died in war, at twenty-eight) would unquestionably have done. Nevertheless, he was a finely gifted individual poet, no more to be designated one of the Georgians than is W. B. Yeats.

Edward Thomas was born of Welsh parents, his father being a clerk in the Board of Trade, at Lambeth, in 1878. Outwardly he was the normal child and boy, taking part in the usual games and occupations; he liked exploring the near-by countryside on the edge of London and particularly enjoyed holidays with relations in Wiltshire. After being at two or three schools he went up to Oxford, where he read History as a non-collegiate student; later he was awarded a scholarship. While still an undergraduate he married Helen, daughter of James Ashcroft Noble, who had encouraged Thomas in his early nature-writing for magazines, etc., and had helped him to get the articles published as *The Woodland Life* in 1897. His early marriage and the fact that he had already decided on a literary career led to some difficulties, especially with his conscientious father. Material difficulties increased during the years that followed, when the Thomases lived in London, Kent, Hampshire. The money he earned by reviewing and by (mostly) commissioned books was never enough to keep off anxiety. There were three children. But despite the melancholia that frequently and for long periods oppressed him, he worked hard, often on material uncongenial to him. Book after book was published; he became 'known'. Edward Garnett, Walter de la Mare, W. H. Davies, Lascelles Abercrombie, Gordon Bottomley, Rupert Brooke, W. W. Gibson, John Freeman, W. H. Hudson are among the people he knew and corresponded with; he was also a friend of Conrad. He walked much in the southern counties of England and in Wales, and not by day only; perhaps it was Kent, Sussex, Wiltshire, Hampshire, and parts of Wales and Gloucestershire that he knew best. He had always been deeply interested in poetry, and had reviewed a great deal of it, but it was not until 1914 that, urged by the American poet Robert

11

EDWARD THOMAS

Frost, he began seriously to write it. He enlisted in 1915.
He did not succeed in placing any of his poems with any
of the likely London editors, but a very small number
found publication mainly through the offices of his painter-
friend, James Guthrie. However, before leaving for
France early in 1917, he made arrangements for the
publication of some sixty-four of his poems; they came out
a few months after he was killed at Arras in April 1917.
In 1918, a further seventy-one poems were published, and
in the *Collected Poems* (Faber and Faber, 1928) there are
one hundred and forty poems; one more poem was added
in the fifth impression of the *Collected Poems* in 1949. R. P.
Eckert's book, *Edward Thomas: a Biography and a Bibliography* (J. M. Dent and Sons, 1937), supplies an abundance of detail about the life and the publications.

The all-over impression that one gathers from examining the majority of the judgments and opinions given
on Thomas from 1917 onwards seems to me to be quite
incommensurate with his worth. With certain notable
exceptions he has been seen mainly as a simple poet
writing of simple things and of simple joys and sorrows, as
a balm for the distressed, as an accurate describer of
beauty in the English countryside. But although he has
been much praised for bareness and simplicity, many
critics have been worried or puzzled by his form, or rather
by the lack of it, by his failure to provide the more usual
kinds of music and metres. Especially was this so in the
early days: here was a poet who somehow did not fit in
with Late Victorian and Georgian modes. But despite this
uneasiness, critic after critic has grouped him, because
of his subject-matter and his 'simple charm', with the
Georgians. Some of the prose books, particularly those
containing the more exalted flights, have received high
praise here and there from Thomas's admirers. But as far

as I know, the prose as a whole has never been given the attention due to it.

Thomas is, of course, in the poetry anthologies, but the effect of his inclusion is, on the whole, to suggest that he is just another pleasant nature poet. Usually he is scantily represented, as half an hour spent at the shelves of any library will readily prove. It may well be true, as S. P. B. Mais says in *A Chronicle of English Literature*, that Thomas 'is best remembered by "Adlestrop" '. *The Progress of Poetry*, by I. M. Parsons, is exceptional among anthologies in treating Thomas as an important modern poet. The majority of histories of literature, including those published in quite recent years, give Thomas summary treatment. It seems obvious that there is a considerable weight of opposition or inertia to be combated in the endeavour to bring about a wide recognition of the status that has so far been given him only by a small body of 'advanced opinion'.

An essential part of the 'legend' is that which celebrates Thomas as having thrown off his self-distrust and indecisiveness when he entered the army, and finding serenity and fulfilment. 'With regular army life,' writes R. P. Eckert, 'his melancholy and dark agonies disappeared for ever.' E. S. P. Haynes wrote in an *English Review* (1917) that 'Edward Thomas died instantaneously in the knowledge that all was well with the cause for which he was fighting'. Thomas Seccombe in a letter to the *Times Literary Supplement* in 1917 said that Thomas's 'dedication' 'electrified some of his friends. They said, "This man was a born soldier".' Mr John Moore, in his *Life and Letters of Edward Thomas* (Heinemann, 1939), says: 'He had changed his whole attitude to life, shaken hands with the past and shut his eyes to the future, so that he was troubled neither with regrets nor apprehensions.' And Lloyd George, in a

Foreword to Mr Moore's book, affirmed that it was war that released the poetic flow; 'all was well from then on', he assures us, seeing in Thomas's life and poetry a grand success story, 'the winning through of an obscure youth to triumph and renown'.

In my opinion these statements are quite naïve in their assumption that 'all was well from then on'. It is true that some of the letters that belong to this period do declare a new-found security and even happiness; but apart from the fact that Thomas wrote to certain of his relations and friends with a tact and a consideration for their feelings, there are many letters which express a condition as different as can be from a sense of well-being. Moreover, one would think that anyone who had read the poetry would hardly find its author the sort of man to undergo an easy conversion: there is no short-cut for anybody, least of all for a man of the sincerity, the seriousness, and the intelligence of Thomas. And could there be a more astonishing remark, bearing in mind the poetry, which he seems to have been writing almost up to the time of his death, than the one to the effect that he had 'shaken hands with the past and shut his eyes to the future'? It was precisely during those last two or three years that his life-long 'concern' with time came to its deepest and finest expression. Those who, for reasons more or less patriotic, or because they like to believe that Thomas did find 'happiness' at the last, or because something disturbing in the poetry makes them glad to turn to what has the appearance for them of a more normal and comforting phase in the poet's life, or for whatever other reason, are eager to emphasize the soldier aspect, are doing no service to the man or the poet. Thomas was not in need of the additional glory that death in war is commonly supposed to confer. And though he was fighting on the same side as, say, Lloyd George, his sense of duty was not at all like the statesman's, nor was he fighting for the same things. It was more relief than joy that Thomas found in a life of routine and obedience to orders, and I believe even that could not have lasted long: a nature like his does not for long escape from itself, whatever gladness it may feel at having escaped from whatever personal worries and vexations. We cannot say whether Thomas would have written the tragic poetry that can spring from a full exposure to life, or whether in fact he would have been able to do what it was Isaac Rosenberg's expressed intention to do: 'I will not leave a corner of my consciousness covered up, but saturate myself with the strange and extraordinary new conditions of this life.' It is possible that a later poetry by Thomas might have shown a controlled fullness that would have justified us in speaking of 'security' or even 'serenity'; I do not think we can say more than that it is possible. And in any case we should not then be dealing with the sort of fulfilment claimed for him with hasty optimism by some of his admirers.

The kind of appreciation that it is the aim of the present book to give will show, I hope, an Edward Thomas who is both finer as a poet and more interesting as a man than the legend and the literary histories suggest. It is nothing like enough—in fact, it is almost beside the point—to praise Thomas for 'quiet, faithful transcriptions' of nature; he has his own vision of nature to convey. And those who chiefly find in him a balm for 'restless and divided hearts' are probably those who normally look for such a balm in all poetry. The beauty that Thomas provides goes with a subtlety and a clarity of mind, and those who stop at the point of emphasizing the 'balm' and his 'exquisite world of simple things' (which are, of course, most beautifully there in his writing) are missing the depth in him which makes his 'simple things' so profoundly different from (say) those of Rupert Brooke in *The Great Lover*. It is in the main the simplicity-lovers who tend to find Thomas's poetry uncertain in form and to deplore his lack of regularity in metre and rhythm. I shall hope to show that the apparent looseness of form is in fact only apparent, that this form is actually the indication of the poet's sure and delicate control of his material and that at its best it is 'inevitable'.

I believe that the best of Thomas's prose, like his poetry, has not had the general recognition it deserves. (I believe also that some sections of it have been overpraised.) There is a quantity of nature writing of the kind that reveals a man of extraordinary gifts. There is some interesting 'miscellaneous' prose. There is a considerable amount of literary criticism that is worth anybody's attention. Those who know the poetry are likely to find something interesting on almost any page of the prose. But it should immediately be added that some sections of it are easily exhausted and would not be read more than once if we were not already interested in Edward Thomas.

Anyone endeavouring to give a full impression and assessment of Thomas the man and the writer is without the advantage of having a number of masterpieces to consider. For he wrote no prose masterpieces, and he is 'only' a very fine minor poet; and there are no very significant 'phases' that can be singled out for treatment. So the method of this book will be, while making the necessary discriminations especially among the prose works, to concentrate on the three or four aspects which seem to me the essential ones. A glance at the *Contents* will show what these are. The second chapter is headed 'Prose', but it is primarily prose that will be dealt with in all chapters until the last is reached. The culmination of Thomas's writing is, as everyone knows, in the poetry; it is there that his mind and spirit are most finely present. To explore and define that mind and spirit, to indicate what particular value they may have for us, is the ultimate aim of this book.

CHAPTER TWO

The Prose

MUCH of the considerable prose output of Edward Thomas (see Appendix) was hack-work, and as such was irksome to the author. He was apt frequently to see himself as a journalist: 'Journalism is as tedious and meaningless as clerk's work,' he wrote to Hudson, 'and, unlike that, cannot be escaped from. It fills *my* normal days from 10 a.m. to 12 p.m., and haunts me all the other days.' *The Life of the Duke of Marlborough*—to give one of many such references—was 'a wretched summer task', involving as it did a large amount of time spent in the British Museum Library, out of the sun and rain. Yet there were times when he could see it in another light: in *The South Country*, when the narrator in the course of a conversation complains that the collar is never off his neck as a hack-writer, the clerk retorts, 'Ah, but it is open to you to do good or bad. We could only do bad.' And though this thought could not have been much of a source of comfort to Thomas, it is a fact that there is good writing in the hack-work, as there is middling and bad writing in the work he chose to do or that had a subject he liked. We should have expected that *The Icknield Way*, which necessitated a lot of walking, would have been a congenial task (despite the kind of work he had to do for a fifty-page chapter called 'History, Myth, Tradition, Conjecture, and Invention'—one imagines a wry smile in the penning of that headline); but there is internal evidence enough, in the repetitive-

ness, in the enumeration of unimportant details, in the
sometimes unnecessarily bitter ironic touches and tone,
that the writing of the book was, in fact, wearisome.
Nevertheless, Thomas is unduly self-deprecatory when he
says in the Dedication to it that what was to have been
a country book 'has turned out to be another of those
books made out of books founded on other books'. *The
Icknield Way* is not as second-hand as that comes to.

The year that Thomas went up to Oxford, was 1897
not a promising time for anybody, and especially un-
propitious for a young man of his particular gifts. He had
already had published a small nature book which was
certainly not 'another of those books made out of books
founded on other books', and now he came into the atmo-
sphere which we epitomize as *fin de siècle* or The 'Nineties,
with its flashiness and its superficial paradox-making, its
parade of languorous and 'aesthetic' attitudes, its literary
practices and preferences unconducive to freshness of outlook and sincerity in living. It seems certain that without
that immersion Thomas would not have developed to
such an extent a prose that owed so much to other writers
—to Wilde, Ruskin, Sir Thomas Browne, Pater, and
others—nor have continued to write it, on and off, for so
long. That is, he might have 'discovered himself' sooner—
an ambiguous expression, I realize, at the best of times,
and particularly so in the case of Thomas, who was always
and consciously 'seeking himself'; I mean that he might
either have written with a more continuous certainty and
power in prose—not necessarily nature writing only—or
have come to poetry a few years earlier than he did. But
conjecture is only conjecture; and what we actually have,
taken as a whole, is of extraordinary interest. And one of
the most interesting things about the prose is the way in
which it shows something of the writer's struggle through

an accumulation of themes, thoughts, attitudes, stylistic devices, towards sincerity, the sincerity of vision and expression that the artist has to win. Thomas was a long time reaching that; he didn't necessarily reach it by discarding showiness and artifice and coming to the more direct writing, good as it is, of much of (say) *The Last Sheaf*, *The Happy-Go-Lucky Morgans*, *The Childhood of Edward Thomas*, or the biographical and critical books. Though that greater directness and simplicity do in this instance indicate an advance.

The 'fine' prose—it is mostly in the five books grouped at the beginning of the Appendix, and more sporadically in the nature books, and in *Oxford*—has received a deal of praise. One knows, however, that the prose in general is very little read, even when it is comparatively accessible. Excerpts appear from time to time in anthologies, and his books are here and there in public libraries. I have found that the more specifically topographical ones are moderately widely read, as belonging to a popular *genre*. For what the information is worth, when I had to get *The South Country*—one of the more popular books, I should say —from a Somerset County Library in a large town, I found it had been taken out eighteen times in twelve years; from the same library *A Literary Pilgrim in England* had been out once in ten years. This last is one of the least interesting of Thomas's books, but one feels that many more people would read it at least once if the name of Thomas were as known as it should be. Mr Roland Gant's selection, *The Prose of Edward Thomas* (The Falcon Press, 1948), has helped to extend that knowledge.

In 1910 *The Times* reviewed *Rest and Unrest*: 'All these . . . sketches and impressions have at least one thought, one feeling in common—the love of all things simple and pure and childlike; the hatred of all things mean, stereotyped, pretentious. They are all the work of a mind as sensitive to beauty as a child, and as consciously critical of beauty as an artist. Filled with that mystical haunting sense that time's defeat of all men's works and ventures is yet somehow the triumph of his inmost desires and imagination—time placid, impalpable, closely heaping its ages over a world mossed like a stone, and yet leaving youth undimmed and beauty undefiled. It is a simplicity, whether of innocence or of wisdom, that most attracts him. Beauty and tenderness. These strangely individual, intensely quiet stories.' And in his Introduction to the Gregynog Press edition of Thomas's *Selected Poems* (1927) Edward Garnett writes: 'Many score of his prose pages, notably in *Rest and Unrest, Light and Twilight, The South Country*, are filled with passages of haunting loveliness, the impressions of a creative, brooding mind and eye sensitive to infinite shades of beauty in the life of the English countryside.' In an article for *The Athenaeum* (1920), he had spoken of *Light and Twilight* as 'the fine flower of Celtic magic'. Of the same work R. P. Eckert says: 'Unquestionably Thomas's finest prose is to be found in this book', and speaks of its 'haunting loveliness, a beauty and sadness of words' which express 'the creative impulse of a poet'.

Judgments of this kind spring in the main from a too easy and willing surrender to the surface glamour of the writing—this is not to say that the writing is nothing but surface glamour—and while one is glad of the praise one cannot but wish that it were less vague and general. When Mr Moore, in his book on Thomas, speaks of 'those brief exquisite pieces of prose' (in *Rest and Unrest* and *Light and Twilight*) as being 'the attempt, falling just short of perfection, at that which in his poetry he perfectly achieved', we may justly expect to be told just how they do fall short and to be given at least a hint of what it was that was perfectly achieved in the poetry. Garnett had previously offered, in *The Athenaeum*, much the same idea of the relationship of this prose to the poetry: 'The beauty of the spiritual vision which inspired the poems was fully revealed, years back, in *Rest and Unrest* and *Light and Twilight*.' That 'fully revealed' forces us to conclude that Garnett failed to perceive the essential nature of the poetry; and several subsequent writers on Thomas have taken their cue from Garnett. Those who find such excellence in the 'poetical' and 'exquisite' prose would seem to have behind them the nineteenth-century idea of poetry—the generalization is permissible here—as pleasant cadences, verbal music approximating to 'magic', dream and other-worldliness, enchantment. An approach conditioned by such an idea can hardly lead to the recognition that the very much finer technique of the poems is the expression of a correspondingly finer grasp of experience. Even the best of the 'fine' prose, with all its undoubted interest, is a *radically* different kind of writing from the poetry. An estimate that is loosely generous is likely in the long run to defeat its own object. Edward Thomas in his prose as in his poetry deserves our best critical attention; there is no danger of his fading into the light of common day.

Sometimes Thomas's prose is little more than the effect of a self-conscious literariness. But even in this, the derivative and the overwritten, there are elements that are present consistently enough to suggest something of the Thomas we know from the poetry, of his interests, themes, feelings, moods, sympathies, and antipathies. From a reading of this section of his prose a man of character and unusual gifts emerges. But what we have is ultimately quite unlike the 'vision' expressed with economy in the poetry.

One of the chief impressions we are likely to carry away from this prose is that of a man with something to say but impeded from satisfying utterance by a strong inclination towards a style of managed effects. Thomas came to be highly skilled in this management, and the effects may come together to make a real beauty of sound and cadence. (We shall be wise, as I hope will sufficiently be shown later, not to condemn out of hand the insincerity that 'managed effects' is bound to imply.)

The poorest of the essays—on the whole they are the earliest—are irritating in their typical essay-like manner and approach, showing palpably the effects of reading Lamb, Wilde, Pater, and others. They have affected archaisms of the 'I have been fain' kind; there are several 'amber fervid evenings'. French and Latin quotations and classical names are plentifully strewn about, as are references to English writers and writings. Sometimes the descriptions are in the main a composite of literary memories and echoes, as here of Tennyson, Wilde, Shelley, Keats:

> Before us lay a broad estuary—moon-enriched, and presently like an even silver trencher, with tree shadows upon it like islets of ebony. A little starry rivulet flowed past us. And on one hand a long road wound upward, shining white, to the top of a hill, and then—the moon, with all her stars.

Sometimes he aggrandizes with a solemnity which even when it is half-mocking is in reality trivial, as when, writing of a shadowy corner in a wood remembered from childhood, he says:

> A dim solitude thus circumscribed liked us hugely. We loved not the insolent and importunate splendours of perfect light.

Yet even in the first book of essays we are likely to meet at any moment something like the following, where despite the hyperbole and eloquence—the sentence is the last of an essay, and he is writing of the effect upon him of the words 'Horae Solitariae'—we feel, especially at the concluding lines and when he speaks of the trees and age, a hint of something strange and individual in the apprehension:

> It has spoken to me in the fields or under the forest, and has a special blessing in the silences of autumn—by day, when the trees seem to have reached great age all at once, seem in truth to be the oldest things on earth, and yet to smile;—by night, when the moon grows lonelier and lonelier in the chill, blue spaces overhead, when the noise as of immense wings quaking at the horizon almost ceases, and the only sound is one leaf justling with another in an overcrowded grave, or, most silent of all sounds, a swallow passing in the darkness.

Sounds and silence, or more accurately sound-and-silence, and solitariness, are to mean much in the consciousness and writing of Thomas; but it would not be unjust to say that as yet his first interest, as evinced in writing of this kind, is in the cadences of an elaborated sentence. He is still in the stage when he can write (in another essay of the same volume), with a mingling of sincerity and affectation, passages like:

> I seemed to be on the eve of a revelation. I could have wept that my senses were not chastened to celestial keenness, to understand the pipits as they flew.

In that stage he was unable to give a clear voice to his intuitions; the intuitions themselves were not grasped clearly. Consider this passage, for instance:

> Each evening, just when the first nightjar was skimming the wood, the sedge-warblers began to sing altogether

round the pool. The song might have been the abstract voice of some old pain, feebly persistent. It went far into the night with a power of ghostly alarms, and attuned to such thoughts as come when night in certain places is malign, reverses the sweet work of day, and gives the likeness of a dragon to the pleasant corner of a wood. The birds were full of prelusive dark sayings about the approaching night. (*Horae Solitariae*)

Thomas is injecting into the song, perhaps with Hardy's aid, significances that are not there, bringing too much of the human world of thought into the birds' world. The large vague terms—'some old pain', 'prelusive dark sayings'—burden the song with an all-too-human ominousness.

Nevertheless, there is an odd sort of sincerity in his portentousness: the intuition is 'unswifted' as it were, by the writer's craft, but the exigencies of the 'impressive' style seldom succeed in smothering, though they blur, an original perception or feeling. Here is a passage from *The Heart of England*:

Far away a gate is loudly shut, and the rich blue evening comes on and severs me irrevocably from all but the light in the old wood and the ghostly white cow-parsley flowers suspended on unseen stalks. And there, among the trees and their shadows, not understood, speaking a forgotten tongue, old dreads and formless awes and fascinations discover themselves and address the comfortable soul, troubling it, recalling to it unremembered years not so long past but that in the end it settles down into a gloomy tranquillity and satisfied discontent, as when we see the place where we were unhappy as children once. Druid and devilish deity and lean wild beast, harmless now, are revolving many memories with me under the strange, sudden red light in the old wood, and not more remote is the league-deep emerald sea-cave from the storm above than I am from the world.

In this overwriting there is a surface impressiveness of a kind like that of the sedge-warbler passage, and the same tendency to lose the actual in large abstractions—'old dreads and formless awes', and so on. Yet beneath the relatively inflated manner one feels a certain reality, the reality of an uncommon way of apprehending. Moreover, the writing is in its way thoughtful; the musical rhetoric contains several quite deliberately stated thoughts.

The presence of a kind of thought in this writing is one of the things that might have made a reader forecast an advance in Thomas towards something finer and more truly rich than purple prose. In the words quoted below, for instance, there is at least the desire to give individual expression to an original perception and thought; Thomas is trying to say a lot here, and he does not succeed in saying it either forcefully or economically, but the way in which he sees the bare branch (with what it suggests of death) as both pictorially and symbolically reducing the distant stars because it is near to us and suggestive of suffering, is potentially that of a poet:

> . . . the eloquence, as of an epigram rich in anger and woe, of one bare branch that juts out from a proud green wood into the little midnight stars and makes them smaller with its splendid pang. (*The Heart of England*)

'Splendid pang' has the falsity of commonplace rhetoric, and the writing might be condemned as the elaboration of a sentimental attitude. But it is not slick, and it seems to me that the way of seeing that it reveals is unusual enough to make us pause.

A later chapter will deal with Thomas's response to the natural world, to speak for the moment in the broadest terms; but reference may suitably be made here to his 'weather consciousness', which is apparent on page after page of the prose. He was extraordinarily aware and observant of weather. The following passage is given, not as one of his best, but to show how that awareness comes through to us in spite of poeticisms and clichés and showy imagery here and there. It is from 'Isoud' in *Cloud Castle*:

> With sunset a vigorous gale took flight from the north, and overthrew the barriers of day and uplifted the heavens a league higher, until the storm came, preceded, while it was yet light, by a wonderful stir and freshness of the air between those heaving bergs of cloud immersed and reluctantly smouldering in blue sky water east and west; and this was the hour for the unexpected, the marvellous, for the extending of Nature's bounds. A moment or two of sumptuous calm—as if one slept upon pillows of wild hop-blossom; the waterfall's breath ceased to tease the ivy foliage, and the storm whipped it instead. Thunder came, and a wind that plucked out the poplar boughs as if they had been hen feathers. That, too, gave way with rumblings of retreat: and the rain was globed prettily on the silver underside of a leaf that lay stiff. So the latest memory of that day was powerful and sweet. We saw the mighty motion of the steadfast tide as it swerved, swerved slowly in echelon at the broadest point of the river, where two streams, both voices of the sea, though querulous, enter it; we saw how the water, all red in the recurrent ardours of sunset, was burdened with foam; how the low grassy shore hissed, and the big, tawny moon leant at watch—as if with a pensive arm—on the hills, quite near. That night also passed, the perfect silence of it expounded by the unaccountable murmur as of gigantic pinions beating slowly at the horizon, and the black bars of midnight weighing heavily upon the brow, until the white moon was deluged by fiery clouds of dawn. Importunate sunlight then called us forth early to a long day of breezes that drove the lark giddily back-

ward in its song. With an imposing promise of the far away spring, a great poplar, in a spurt of delicate rain, rose up in magically aggrandized magnificence into a lustrous pane of sky.

Enough actuality can be extracted from even this heightened writing to make good the claim for the author of an unusual and a sharp interest in the phenomena he is dealing with.

Immediately following that passage comes the story, told in a rather affected archaic-simple manner, of Isoud and Kehydius: 'but most impressively the memory of that day is inseparable from a reading of Malory's narrative of the bright Kehydius'. The comparative clumsiness of the transition to the mediaeval and idyllic need not concern us, but it is interesting to consider the fact that a mingling or a simple juxtaposition of the actual with the literary-derived and the historic-romantic is a characteristic feature of many of the essays.

The *Morte d'Arthur* was one of those books—another was *The Compleat Angler* ('the sweetness and antiquity of England')—which for a long time were to Thomas a kind of symbol or picture of a perfection and a beauty beyond that of the actual present. We could readily collect thirty romantic essays from his work, romantic in their pre-occupation with the desire for lost Edens, and extending over a period of some fifteen years; he was still writing them when he was past thirty. But his romanticism was not that of the best-seller in prose or poetry, which passes off falsification of fact and actuality as truth, whether through self-deception or by design. It is true that his 'dream' often attracts him powerfully, and that he indulges in feelings and attitudes which, as he himself is likely to point out, can't reasonably be justified. But a certain self-awareness is almost always evident; the conclusion of 'On the Evenlode' (*Horae Solitariae*) shows it at its simplest and most explicit:

> Before noon I left, with a plan of soon returning. But the next day passed, and several more. When at last I went, my flowers from that sweet place had withered. A friend accompanied me. I need say no more. The river is branched and serpentine just there, and we searched in vain. Even I sometimes think there never was such a farmhouse and St Cecilia, though in my dreams it is otherwise.

On more than one occasion Thomas referred to his 'lies in print', and though we shall not wholly accept that valuation, having in mind his habitual self-belittlement, we know he was deeply dissatisfied with much of what he wrote. It is interesting, especially in the light of what was to come later, to look at certain manifestations of the romanticism which was undoubtedly what he had chiefly in mind when he spoke of his lies in print.

The mood of the writing under immediate consideration is often reminiscent and nostalgic. 'Home', in *Light and Twilight*, has the stereotyped situation of the soldier dying abroad and calling up memories of a childhood journey with his father from London to Wales:

> They stopped again where there was only a black-bearded, tall man and a sheep-dog waiting. They could hear the thrushes sing, under the clear blue and the lightless moon, from out of dark thickets in a hollow, rushy land, backed by the sea and the orange sails of vessels that caught the dawn. 'Over there,' said his father, 'is the land we have come from.' It was as faint and grey and incredible in the distance as his own land was clear and true; and he sighed with happiness and security, and also with anticipation of the further deeps that were to be revealed, the battlefield, the curlew's eggs, the castles, the harps, the harpers harping all the songs of his father.

Here we feel something of freshness and actuality with the note of longing. At other times there is a languor that is mostly a literary pose; Pater and Tennyson are most palpably present here:

> For a little while, troubled tenderly by autumnal maladies of soul, it was sweet and suitable to follow the path towards our place of rest,—a gray, immemorial house with innumerable windows. (*Rose Acre Papers*)

We shall see that writing like this—'Everywhere, the languid perfumes of corruption', he says in the same essay, 'An Autumn House'—represents more in Thomas than a purely professional exploitation of *fin-de-siècle* attitudes.

Imaginings of idyllic regions are often presented expressly as the effect of the desire for something better than this earth can give. Here is part of a city clerk's dream, inspired by his hearing a tune played in the street. He has 'a pale spectacled face, dark eyes and moustache, and a look of vacant solemnity and virtue':

> The air was clear, and the light of an unearthly purity, like the air and light of imaginary lands in poems and impossible tales. There was nowhere any sign of decay or change. The sea was innocent. The sun could not set off from the islands and waters, for it hung aloft for ever in obedient majesty. All things expressed a calm and certainly immortal bliss.
>
> What seemed at first another island floating upon the laughing water was a ship, worthy of the utmost pomp of Cleopatra. It was overgrown with flowers and leaves, so as to be known for a ship only by its motion and its high, extravagant prow and stern as it advanced slowly among the islands. While it glided, music arose: and the music seemed that of the innumerable flowers spiring up or floating down from the exuberant foliage, so soft was it, and of such a nimble and thoughtless kind; and the swaying and onward rising of the vessel was beautiful of itself, as if it were wafted by the music. Birds

flitted among that foliage also, and scattered without diminishing the blossoms.

The essay from which that is taken, namely 'Barque d'Amour' in *Light and Twilight*, shows Thomas sharing the clerk's dream and at the same time being well aware that it is a dream: 'imaginary lands in poems and impossible tales', he says; and at the end, the clerk 'looked up at the office clock, and its two hands together at five minutes past one'. But the reference to 'poems and impossible tales' is in part defensive, and the perfection of spontaneity represented by that particular kind of music, 'nimble and thoughtless' (which was what the clerk, and the writer, were not) was something that Thomas perhaps never ceased to wish for, though it is clear that the mind that produced the poetry is one that has confronted itself with the quality and worth of its previous transcendental hopes and fancies.

One can imagine an approach that would make a good deal out of Thomas's frequent and lengthy descriptions of young women and maidens who may be said in general to be watery amalgams of certain of Jefferies' heroines and the Lucy of 'Three years she grew', not forgetting the ladies of ancient legends and stories: nearly all of them lack robustness of actuality and real spiritual quality. The psychologists would be wrong, I think, to see more significance in these than in Thomas's charmed islands and ships and castles. The rapture with which they are described is of the managed and literary kind; it is never an excitement due to causes of which the writer is unconscious. The immaturity is not that of the simpleton sublimating his sexuality in idealistic language. The St Cecilias and Isouds belong with the islands and magic barques as types of perfection sought half with fervour and half with scepticism.

Sometimes his writing on this theme is very bad: it is a very stale sort of ecstasy, with its piled-up classical and literary allusions, that is expressed in the long last paragraph of 'The End of a Day' in *Light and Twilight* (an essay that has been singled out for praise by more than one critic). The following is one of many excerpts that could be given to show the kind of idealization we are dealing with; it is from 'The Fountain' (*Rest and Unrest*):

> If a brook might attain in a human form the embodiment of its purity, coldness, light, and desire to be ever moving, of its mysterious transformations in clouds of heaven and in caves under the rocks, it would be in such a form as hers. The gravity, the dark simplicity, above all the exquisite combination of wildness and meekness in the girl would be worthy of the most sacred fountain, whether emerging among moss and crags and the shadows of crags or among sunlit grass. Surely, I thought, a lymph of crystal ran in her veins. It was the darkness of a hidden spring that chilled her pellucid brow. The radiance of her eyes, her face, her whole form, was of the dawn, which I dreamed she was one of the few left to worship—Yes! She had listened to the nightingales when the dew and the hawthorn flower and the young grass were yet dark; and the thrill of their songs had entered her eyes and lips without one passionate or confusing thought.

The whole of the account of the meeting with the girl on the sea-shore is in this vein; the inflation is nowhere checked by self-questioning. It is true that the girl is seen for a moment only, before she disappears, and this may be the author's comment on her possibility. But even if you take the whole thing symbolically, the exaltations are so stereotyped that whatever is symbolized is quite without significance. And when R. P. Eckert says: 'In *The Fountain* is expressed his recognition of the spiritual beauty

THE PROSE

within all life ... the one-ness of time and eternity', he is
merely making the vaguest of gestures and failing to be a
good reader. Mr Eckert's book is a most valuable one, and
will be consulted with gratitude by all those who are
interested in Thomas, but it seems to me to fail whenever
it comes to consider, whether or not with the help of
Garnett and others, the actual writings. To him 'The
Fountain' is remarkable for 'unity and strength'. I think
most readers would be more likely to speak of weakness,
and to conclude that when the Olwens and Bronwens become Helens and goddesses and Guineveres, it is half because they answer vaguely to some desire in Thomas for
an ideal perfection, and half because he has to write so
many words in a given time at the command of his
circumstances.

A complementary feeling to that brand of idealism or
rapture is wistfulness; there is sadness at loss, at non-
fulfilment. Thomas has many tales and incidents where
the pathos is very thin and which, if it were not for the
touches of fresh perception scattered through them, we
could well consign to the stock Victorian-pathetic. The
little girl who is drowned while gathering flowers; Alice
Lacking, the young woman growing into middle age with
memories of past happiness, and after an illness deciding
to adopt a child no one wants; a group of down-and-outs
sitting on seats in a London park: these and similar subjects gave Thomas opportunities for an indulgence which,
though we cannot say the opportunities were eagerly and
excitedly grasped and though the indulgence was rarely
gross, could have done nothing towards enlarging and
deepening his experience. To say, as many have, that
'The Flower Gatherer', 'The First of Spring', 'A Group of
Statuary', are 'beautifully written' is to indicate nothing,
for the writing is of the accomplished kind that overlays

the feeling which was its ostensible inspiration, and the final effect has too much of manufacture about it to be pathetic.

In the phase of Thomas's prose with which we are at present concerned—not a chronological phase, let us remember—among the most interesting pages, especially to those who have some knowledge of Thomas the poet, are those for which the best word (for the moment) is 'impressionistic'. And the impressionism is romantic in that it has to do with themes that are normally so called and with moods that are usually of simple regret and simple yearning. There are waste lands where snow drifts down for ever; castles at the sea's edge or in the mountains, so old that they are indistinguishable from the crags on which they are built; princesses dying young, and men on quests; islands that appear and disappear through the mists; all this, and never far away the people of the *Morte d'Arthur*, and Tennyson's gloomy shores, and Swinburne's cliff-ledge gardens. Yet it isn't altogether a matter of emotional simplicities and literary derivativeness; something more than an effete and melodramatic romanticism is conveyed, for instance, in writing like the following; it is from 'Snow and Sand' (*Rest and Unrest*):

> The sand is hissing about her hair, but she cannot hear it; it is poured into the room like water. For the wind has filled itself with sand as but a little while before it filled itself with the gold of sunset and the scent of the rose; and the heavy billows of the sand are drowning the sea-birds. The princess cannot hear the wrath of the sea any more than if she had eyes she could see it, through the sandstorm, baying at the foot of the tower. She cannot feel the sand rising above her waist. She cannot cry out or fly; she has no desire or motion. There is not one left in the castle to cry out to her or to come to her door; for some have broken forth to die in the sea, and some have drunk the sand and have died like her

amid the mist and hiss of the floating and whirling dunes. The tower plunges through the solid air into the black sea and buries the corpse of the betrothed. The wind blows her dust into my face as it shakes the drab grass on the last stones of the tower. It is an old wind. A minute ago it had forgotten such a little thing as the tempest of sand and sea, the overthrow of the tower, the maiden's death, and her black hair spread out by the slow wave. But now it has remembered as it whirls the sand and the crossing flakes of snow together, above the ruins of the tower, the drab grasses, the homeless dunes. There is nothing else to do but to remember here. It is a sea of solid waves, of sand hills that behold the mountains, the sea and the sky, and of sand valleys that behold only the sand hills and the sky. Some of the hills are stony grey or brown with dead bracken, some of the valleys yellow-green with moss and with moss-like turf, or grey with the sprawling roots and the flaked leaves of little willows. But most are bare of all but the corpse tresses of yellow grass, and the wind carves ceaselessly and erases its carving, and in small hollows bows the pointed stem of the grass and guides it so as to draw a circle upon the sand. Many skeletons of birds lie on the sand, but there is not a bird in the air, no sound but the shifting of the grains as the wind broods. There is nothing but change, unresting, monotonous change. The wind is counting the sands and going over memories which are of the sands. . . .

And in this vein the writing continues, and goes on to tell of a house that formerly stood near by, and of a couple living there, and of the man shooting one of the myriad white birds that wheeled and wailed everlastingly over the lake in the valley. It would be easy to dismiss it all as 'decadent': the induced mood of regretful brooding with its elaborating on decay, the eloquence which is mainly a matter of repetitions and cadences (with effects that may remind us of things like Morris's

Round the lone house in the midst of the corn.
Speak but one word to me over the corn,
Over the tender, bow'd locks of the corn),

the very thin "Lady of Shalott" type of pathos. But with all this conceded, the flow of the writing is not just fluency covering vacuity; something of a mood that is not entirely induced is conveyed by the sound and movement of the words, as in a poem that is mainly dependent upon onomatopoeia and yet represents something 'real' in the author. (Tennyson, in particular, comes to mind.) There are, moreover, touches of actuality: he has watched and listened to the movements of sand and seen the effect of the wind which 'in small hollows bows the pointed stem of the grass and guides it so as to draw a circle upon the sand'. But mostly he is consciously aiming at evoking a trance-like state, 'listening to the two gentle dissolving murmurs of the gliding sand and the kissing flakes, sounds that are taking possession of all things as of me, so that in all the drowsy world there seems nothing but the formless mazy snowfall and the vague changing dunes'. Those words are interesting in what they suggest of the peculiar *absorption*, seeming to amount to temporary loss of identity, which played a part in forming the total experience given in the poetry. But perhaps the most cogent thing to say here about the kind of writing we are considering is that it deals with time, with the work of time, and that he too readily and easily enlists the falling towers, the sand and sea and the maidens, to convey the sense of transcience which we know was always with him. There is no personal urgency in the writing; he is, in fact, getting away from his deepest self, half-hiding from himself the disturbance that his preoccupation with time caused in him, putting it into a fanciful story and an elaborate style, dissolving its force into a mood of wistfulness which at the same time comprehends a delight in the sound of his words. What must (we know) have deeply and sharply concerned him, turns into reverie and music. Later, the poetry will tell us things that this prose cannot.

Thomas was extremely fond of describing the backgrounds and settings of these particular essays, which if they are to be called imaginative and not merely fanciful, are so by virtue of the consistency with which the sense of desolation is conveyed, a gentle and not a sharp desolation. Sometimes the strangeness comes out of a contemplation of the actual, as in the following passage from 'The Island' in *Light and Twilight* (it is an elusive island, always waiting, never landed upon):

> Or a man goes down to the rocks through a soft wind that is all grey rain. A wreath of little birds pipes by and drifts rapidly into nothing. The earth under him is being dissolved into something vague and desolate, into a mist like the sea and sky. A heron detaches itself from the dark rock and pale pool, where it was unseen, and flaps heavily into the enfolding rain without a sound, towards the island, which is invisible before, as the mainland, the beach, the sand wall, the long curve of coast behind are also invisible. He can see nothing but the near rocks, their weedy crevices, the still pools on the shelves, as he climbs and stumbles and zigzags onward and outward, until the gossamer rain seems to begin to shape out of itself a mound—a cone—a shadow —the island—which disappears as it is completed; and out of this the curlews are crying.

One feels that for Thomas the radiant princesses offset to some degree this feeling of transitoriness and insubstantiality. To imagine them was a kind of (short-lived) compensation. Like the mists and towers and islands, they were consciously-sought and consciously-elaborated visions. Later there was to come the 'vision' in which—to understate it—there was still insubstantiality, but which made it unnecessary for that sort of compensation to be sought, because the here-and-now gave so much. Even though it did not give 'happiness'.

As a matter of fact, taking the prose as a whole there is plenty of the here-and-now. And though the things observed, the perceptions, haven't the significance that they have when they come to be incorporated in the full response expressed by the poetry, they do, nevertheless, constitute a kind of reality. When he says, '. . . the jackdaws chaff one another in the clear sky above their wood', we welcome the offered truth of that 'chaff'. When he writes:

> In one place the furze on a mound makes a little world for two or three pairs of linnets and whitethroats, and there are the largest and sweetest blackberries; there also a hundred stems of brier spend spring and summer in perfecting the curves of their long leaps—curves that are like the gush of water over a dam, and yet crossing in multitudes without crowding, in all ways without discord, like the paths of the flight of swallows when they embroider the twilight air. . . . (*The Heart of England*)

we know at least that a remarkably keen eye has been at work. And there is more than the knowledge of a naturalist in his account (from an article written for *Country Life*) of 'flowers of frost' on a stick in the wood; it is the enjoyed sight that I wish to indicate as relevant here, not the Fates and the lightly cynical 'hastily thrown aside':

> Lying over the ivy is what might be the distaff, hastily thrown aside, from which the Fates were spinning the thread of some singularly fortunate, pure life—a distaff as it were bound round the middle with whitest wool. The distaff is a rotten peeling branch of beech, and the wool is a frost flower, such as may be found on any frosty, still day and always attached to a branch like

this. The frost looks as if it had grown out of the dead wood; it is white and glossy, and curled like the under-wool which a shearer exposes on the belly of a sheep when he begins to shear it for the first time; but it is finer than any wool, and the threads, as much as three inches long, are all distinct as if combed.

And in the same article:

Of a different kind is the beauty of the blades of ice that will occasionally be found attached to one side, not necessarily the under side, of every twig on every tree in the wood, and to every dead stem of dock and rag-wort in the neglected fields above. These blades having an even or serrated edge and either as clear as glass or powdered with hoar frost, reach a breadth of an inch or more and almost the thickness of a sword. When it thaws they fall in rustling, jingling, glittering showers, and lie on the earth in fragments that soon melt to-gether into mounds of a tender grey.

The kind of observation revealed in these instances constitutes an actuality as opposed to the 'romance' with which the present chapter has up till now been mainly concerned. Thomas's prose has also many clear accounts of actual people, such as the mole-catcher in his first book, *The Woodland Life*, or 'The Man of the Woods' in *Cloud Castle*, though it cannot be said that such accounts were of primary importance in his writing; the grounds for this statement will be given in the chapter that follows. Also at a far remove from the lady-in-the-tower attitude is a remark like this about Nell, one of the 'Seven Tramps' (*Cloud Castle*): 'She was foolish when drunk, mad when sober, and talked continually at the top note of tragical expression.'

There is much humour scattered about the prose. Thomas can smile at many things, not least at himself, and with various shades and intentions. He is likely to

EDWARD THOMAS

bring in humour with almost any topic, as here (in *In Pursuit of Spring*) where ostensibly he is giving information:

> The end of Ewell touched the beginning of Epsom, which had to be entered between high walls of adver- tisements—yards of pictures and large letters—asserting the virtues of clothes, food, drugs, etc., one sheet, for example, showing that by eating or drinking something you gained health, appetite, vigour, and a fig-leaf. The exit was better.

Four and Twenty Blackbirds, which tells twenty-four stories as the source of the same number of proverbs, is pervaded by a humour which comes from the union of delightful inventiveness with a quiet factual tone. The book was written for children, and here and there the humour seems to be rather too subtle and sophisticated. But here is the beginning, simple enough, of 'A Cat may look at a King':

> David Haggis, King of Scotland, would not let anyone see him without his crown. Therefore he never married, and in his palace all the attendants were blind men. The Taker-off and Putter-on of the crown were both blind men. He would not even see himself with his crown off. He had no mirrors, and instead of water he washed himself in skim milk, which he did because he was too fond of cream to waste it. He was the first king to wash in skim milk.

The early *Oxford* is a book of varying quality and manner, being a guide and a history and something of a personal record, and moving between the extremes of rather commonplace raptures about the 'sweet city' on the one hand, and on the other an almost savage anger at the encroachments on its beauty. Sometimes we have this:

And it is day once more; and beauty, the one thing in Oxford that grows not old, seems a new-born, joyous thing, to a late watcher who looks out and sees the light first falling on dewy spires;

and sometimes this:

But the dark entry to the city, on the western side, suddenly changed my thoughts. It is well known. It is the most contemptible in Europe. It consists of a hoarding, a brewery, and suitable appurtenances. Of more recent date is the magnificent marmalade shop, the most conspicuous building in Oxford. On the north and east the approach is not worse, consisting, as it does, of sermons in brick, arranged in perfectly success-ful imitation of Tooting.

And as if he thought that passage might appear in-ordinately funny to those who prefer Cambridge, he put into *The Icknield Way* a description that ends thus:

. . . fine open cornland northward, lines of trees down its slopes, woods on its ridges, and the tall chimneys of Cambridge six miles away. . . .

and soon afterwards there are 'paper wrappings of sausages . . . thrown out by motorists from Cambridge'. The tone of the humour in *Oxford* is often uncertain, the attitude sometimes superior—it was the Oxford of the turn of the century—but on the whole the humour is happy and pleasant. A youthful facetiousness comes out at times, particularly when he adopts the manner of the seventeenth-century character writers; it seems clear that Thomas was over-impressed by their clever terseness. But his sketches of University types are amusing, and a close perusal of them would show a Thomas who, despite all the smart writing, is exercising a certain shrewdness of observation and finding a pleasure in recording it. Of one of the many dons he writes lightly about, he says:

Perhaps he is in the main a summer bird. Then he shows that he is gallant as well as a scholar and a man of the world. He is the figure-head of his college barge during The Eights, and with an eye-glass, that is a kind of sixth sense, he surveys womankind, and sees that it is good.

And of a type of undergraduate that is well-known:

He acquires the lofty cynicism of the under-informed and the over-fed.

Sometimes the laughter is very much on the wrong side of the face. His dissatisfaction with commercial values takes on a bitterness, beneath the dry statement, when he writes in *The Icknield Way* that sheep

have become more and more a kind of living machinery for turning vegetables into mutton, and only in their lambhood or motherhood are they obviously of a different tribe from sausage machines.

In *Marlborough*, where his view of the Duke's times and campaigns is coolly and consistently disenchanted, there are many passages with a tone like the following:

It became a tedious game, suited particularly to Kings and generals. It was very bloody work, especially for the besiegers, but could be watched in safety by Kings, ladies, and children.

While in this piece from 'Mothers and Sons' (*Rest and Unrest*), his disgust at the pollution is enforced by an ironical quotation and comparison, brought in not altogether necessarily and yet seemingly quite spontaneous and suggesting a further distaste, namely of the hypocrisy of what he sees as the Christmas confusion of animality and spirituality:

One of the rivers was now increased by waste from the chemical works, and the water was of mingled yellow and red that suggested the fat and the lean of carcases in a butcher's shop when 'the time draws near the birth of Christ'. No salmon would face such a flood, but one girl, I was informed, had lately chosen the deep pool where the poison entered to drown herself.

It is the direct freshness of that 'No salmon would face such a flood' which makes that sentence rather savagely humorous and saves it from being merely an echo of the Hardy gloom and cynicism. The juxtaposition of the filthy river and Tennyson's idealism is bitter enough.

The pretentiousness of the self-righteous and of the merely formal was one of the dislikes that Thomas expressed most often; he had a healthy disregard of the religious attitudes and sanctions that are bound up with such pretentiousness:

It has a gray, weedy churchyard, far too large for the few big ivy-covered box tombs lying about in it like unclaimed luggage on a railway platform.

He always looked at the epitaphs in the countless churches and churchyards he visited, and never failed to find something to amuse and to ponder on. The irony of the following, from *In Pursuit of Spring*, comes of his extreme distaste for the glibness of the carved words:

A cottage near the church bore upon its walls these words, cut in stone, before Queen Victoria's time,

> 'Fear God
> Honour the King
> Do good to all men.'

Probably it dates from about the year of Alton Workhouse, from the times when kites and ravens abounded, and thrived on the corpses of men who were hanged for a little theft committed out of necessity or love of sport. The fear of God must have been a mighty thing to bring forth such laws and still more the obedience to them.

Another revealing epitaph incident (in *The Icknield Way*) is refreshing with the sort of irreverence which comes ultimately from a reverence for life; the oddity, the comic gruesomeness are humorous and not simply frivolous, and the feeling behind 'those sweet words' is obviously genuine:

The most notable thing in the church was an oval tablet inscribed with the words:—

Beneath
lie
the remains of
William Turner
Esquire
who died 23rd March
1797 aged 61
'Here the wicked cease
from troubling and
the weary are
at rest.'

The word 'here' my fancy took quite literally, and I saw a skeleton cramped behind the tablet protesting to the living that there inside the wall, denuded of flesh and of all organs, nerves, and desires, a wicked man ceased from troubling and a weary one could be at rest; the teeth of the skeleton shook in their dry sockets as it, a hundred and ten years old, uttered those sweet words: 'Here the wicked cease from troubling and the weary are at rest.'

Later, wishing to escape the rowdy music of a fair, he writes:

The most I could do was to go into a taproom, where the music did not penetrate and the weary were at rest.

There follow humorous-satirical descriptions of the fatuous idealized Victorian female portraits that hung on the walls, and the excessive length and the repetitiveness of these descriptions do, in fact, show a weary Thomas; the long-drawn-out and rather stereotyped satire is an indication of an inner dissatisfaction, a dissatisfaction not to be accounted for by a dislike of silly pictures. Thomas's humour was sometimes a defence: 'against what?' is a question that will be at least partially answered in later chapters.

The portraits in Chapter IV of *Wales*, despite the ways in which they suggest a knowledge, as in *Oxford*, of the works of Earle and Overbury and others, show an agile wit and skill in expressing his understanding of Welsh types; that they are, often, very much types, doesn't preclude insight and a keen good sense. There is Mr Jones, the minister, who

> takes religion, as he does his severe morality, like a sensuous delight. One might think from his epithets that he was an æsthete, except that he is so abandoned. When he ventures to speak of men, their very virtues and vices are all handled in such a way that they seem to be his own imaginations. Thus, his drunkard is as unreal and as terrible as a chimera. . . . It is not, therefore, surprising that at one time he had gorgeous earthly dreams.

There is Owen, the swaggering failure, landlord of the Cross Inn, who,

> had he lost by a bargain, had he taken a bad coin unawares, had he been worsted in argument, could so rant that he moved everyone, and himself obviously first of all, and made the worse appear the better.

There is another minister, Mr Rowlands, a huge man with a huge voice:

> When he reads a lesson, it is plain to see that above all other Gods he loves 'the Lord that smiteth'. He opens

his mouth and rejoices in the rich and massy Welsh. . . . Once he paused long, towards the end of a sermon, while the thunder withdrew with a terrible solemnity which he envied; and he did not hesitate to follow the thunder with the words, 'It has been said', and so to end.

There is the bard, real with a sort of mystic passion, but unreal in the actual world, incapacitated by literariness:

I think he wastes so much pity for Annie of Lochroyan that other maids find him passionless, and he grows tender over Burd Helen and Cynisca as their lovers never did.

And there is the schoolmaster Pugh, living a kind of pseudo-life:

Thus, of old cities, rivers flowing past famous places, mountains of beauty or story, the white cliffs of the south, the whin-red moorland of Wales, old gardens, solemn woods, all solitudes, fading races, sunsets, fallen greatness in men and things, old books, old beer, poverty, childhood . . . of all these he will talk as if he had discovered them to the world, though it may be doubted whether he knows them at all.

But perhaps it is not mainly humour that this last portrait offers: 'It is comic and it is terrible', is Thomas's own comment.

The account which the present chapter gives of the prose is necessarily incomplete. There are significant themes that demand fuller treatment. For in addition to his possessing certain extraordinary qualities of vision, in a more than visual sense, and of sensuous perceptiveness, Thomas was a man who thought much about life. And though this thought is nowhere embodied in great prose, over and over he expresses ideas and incorporates values which enhance both our sense of his fineness and our own sense of life. When he ponders on the effects of what he rather affectedly calls 'the rash burial of rural divinities', on the nature of an old countrywoman's Christianity, on narrowness of living, and frustration, on industry, suburbanism, puritanism, and much more, he is interesting by the quality of his thought as well as by his attitudes. Moreover, out of the observing and the pondering there emerges much of the man who is the author of the poems. It is interesting to see how the meaning, for the Thomas of the prose, of a phrase like 'the annihilating sea and night' is taken up and transformed in the more subtle experience of the poetry; and to discern the characteristic note in the heightened manner of a paragraph like this:

> When I had walked another mile, the wood was out of sight, the thrush unheard. The wood is now purple immortally, for ever that song emerges from its heart, as free from change as one whom we remember vividly in the tip-toe of his exulting youth, and dying then has escaped huskiness, and a stoop, and foul breath, and a steady view of life.

We shall see that life meant intensely to him despite the recurrent note of a weariness that is too often immaculate:

> I suppose that up there also nothing matters but eternity; that up there also they know nothing of eternity.

I do not think there is any prose work of Edward Thomas of which we can say that the quality is sustained. Inside the covers of a book by him we are likely to get different intentions, approaches, styles. Even a nature book with a definite theme is likely to be a mixture of plain reporting, live description, verbose description, strong or delicate feeling, 'literary' feeling, and so on, with uneasy transitions from mood to mood, from subject to subject, from the actual to the 'dream' and back again. But many pages, and many essays, have the interest and the beauty of individual writing: 'The Stile', 'The Moon', 'Mike', 'Insomnia', 'In the Crowd at Goodwood', 'This England', 'London Miniatures', 'Glamorgan', are among the best single essays. Another is 'A Third-class Carriage' (from *The Last Sheaf*, in which most of the above are to be found).

This essay is not only interesting because it shows the attitude and feeling, the values, that we associate with Thomas; it is also in itself clear in intention, forceful, unrepetitive, and vivid. It is not, of course, force and immediacy of the order of Lawrence's or Conrad's that we are dealing with; nevertheless, the writing is firm and clear enough to give the incident something of the force of a metaphor.

The essay begins with the colonel climbing into the carriage:

> When the five silent travellers saw the colonel coming into their compartment, all but the little girl looked about in alarm to make sure that it was a mere third-class carriage. His expression, which actually meant a doubt, whether it was not perhaps a fourth-class carriage, had deceived them.

The child is so mentioned, innocent of snobbery, free from the timidities and terrors that go with the wrong sort of regard for social conventions. The looks and gestures of the other passengers are briefly given and interpreted, as are those of the colonel, who prepares to smoke his pipe. Thomas, with quiet irony, goes some way towards placing him:

> He was restraining his eyes from exercise, well knowing that nothing worthy of them was within range. The country outside was ordinary downland, the people beside him were but human beings.

At the end of the essay we shall be asking, 'But what sort

of a *human* being is he, and the other grown-ups?' Not that
there is any crudity of explicitness in the way he is exposed. As a matter of fact, the colonel's pipe-smoking is
described lovingly; over half the length of the essay he is
built up sympathetically as a connoisseur: 'the dry, bitter-
sweet aroma' was worth all his trouble, and Thomas gives
(romantically, we are likely to think) a certain transcendental value to the colonel's activity:

> To preserve and advance that gleam on the briar, to
> keep burning that Arabian sweetness, was hardly less
> than a vestal ministry.

Nevertheless, though Thomas was fond of smoking, he was
quite unlike the colonel whose 'brain subdued itself lest by
its working it should modify the joys of palate and nostrils'.
And when we come to the climax of the incident—the
child asking the colonel to smell—we shall realize that the
phrase 'the joys of palate and nostrils' is as much irony as
simple truth. The journey continues:

> There was not a sound in the carriage except the
> colonel's husky, mellow breathing.

The little girl has

> a basketful of wild roses on her lap, which she looked
> at when she was not staring out at the long, straight-
> backed green hill in full sunlight, the junipers dappling
> the green slope, and whatever was visible to her
> amongst them.

The colonel does note, despite his condition, the entrance
into the compartment, at the next stop, of

> a pink youth in a white waterproof, brown shoes, and
> hollycock hat, carrying golf-clubs and a suit-case.

He continues smoking.

> Not long afterwards the train stopped at the edge of a
> wood where a thrush was singing, calling out very loud,

clear things in his language over and over again. In this
pause the other passengers were temporarily not content
to look at the colonel and speculate on the cost of his
tobacco, his white waterproof, and his teeth and gold
plate, on how his wife was dressed, whether any of his
daughters had run away from him, why he travelled
third-class; they looked out of the window and even
spoke shyly about the thrush, the reason of the stop,
their destination. Suddenly, when all was silent, the
little girl held up her roses towards the colonel saying:
'Smell.'

The colonel, who was beginning to realize that he was
more than half-way through his pipe, made an in-
describable joyless gesture designed to persuade the
child that he was really delighted with the suggestion,
although he said nothing, and did nothing else to prove
it. No relative or friend was with her, so again she said:
'Smell. I mean it, really.'

Fortunately, at this moment the colonel's eyes fell on
the pink youth, and he said:
'Is Borely much of a place, sir?'

Every one was listening.

'No, sir; I don't think so. The railway works are
there, but nothing else, I believe.'

'I thought so,' said the colonel, replacing his pipe in
his mouth and his mind in its repose. Every one was
satisfied. The train whistled, frightening the thrush, and
moved on again. Until it came to the end of the journey
the only sound in the carriage was the colonel knock-
ing out the ashes of his pipe with a sigh.

When it is suggested that Thomas's essay has something
of the force of a metaphor, the implication is that we are
aware of a significance below the narrative, the descriptions, and the dialogue. That first 'smell', for instance, is
not only effective in its breaking the silence; it hints at a
starvation of instinct and the senses, of the feeling for
beauty, in the colonel and the youth. One would not wish

to labour this point: we are not dealing with a tale by
Lawrence or Henry James. But Thomas does neatly and
firmly communicate his sense of the indifference and in-
sentience that develop in convention-ridden lives; the
colonel, despite his pipe, and the youth, despite his golf-
clubs, cannot because of their snobbery live 'in the now.'
And they are not simply two persons in a railway carriage;
they represent a way of life that Thomas sees as not only
limited and unpleasant but also, we feel, as a disastrous
development: to them, the only thing that may commend
the small English town or village—it's not 'much of a
place'—is the railway works. They are not alone in their
torpor; the other adults do speak 'shyly' of the thrush
(which calls out 'loud, clear things'), but their speculations
are trivial and snobbish, and their fear or obsequiousness
makes them unaware of or at least enables them easily to
put aside the horror of the snub. The child's making it clear
that her offer to share the pleasure is sincere—'I mean it,
really'—adds just a touch of pathos, but being innocent
she is probably unsnubbable, and the horror isn't so much
for what is done to her feelings as for what the whole
incident conveys. 'Horror' is a strong word, but so long
as we do not reserve it for *Macbeth* and *Heart of Darkness* I
think we shall be doing no more than justice to Edward
Thomas to say that he experienced it when he contem-
plated some aspects of the civilization he lived in. Such
a contemplation was not, as most readers will know, his
main subject. But it helped strongly to form his mature
consciousness. In what ways it did so will be discussed
later. At this point it will be more useful to discuss another
'contemplation', a contemplation which was bound up
with his attitude to society, and which was fundamental
in his living as well as being productive of much writing;
this is, of course, his contemplation of Nature.

CHAPTER THREE

Nature and the Country;
and a Comparison

EDWARD THOMAS has the gifts that we expect to find in any good nature writer; and in addition his 'vision' of nature is significant and individual. It is mainly in the poetry that we shall find our justification for speaking of significance, but the quality of mind and personality that come through to us from the prose is such that in certain aspects there is not, I believe, a nature writer in the language who surpasses him.

Thomas tells us that when he was a boy he copied into several of his Jefferies books these words from the end of *The Amateur Poacher*:

> Let us get out of these narrow modern days, whose twelve hours somehow have become shortened, into the sunlight and the pure wind. A something that the ancients thought divine can be found and felt there still.

The words, he says, were a gospel and an incantation to him. Thomas was to find in nature much that was not sunlight and pure wind; but the gospel of Jefferies' words was never for him a romantic enthusiasm in the abstract, it was linked with actuality. He was intensely the 'lover' of nature from his early boyhood. If anyone doubts this, he should read the chapter called 'Our Country' in *The Happy-Go-Lucky Morgans*; the detail to be found there is

abundant warrant that it is not just an idealizing memory
that is at work in a passage like this:

> If we left it unvisited for some weeks it used to appear
> to our imaginations extraordinary in its beauty, and
> though we might be forming plans to go thither again
> before long, I did not fully believe that it existed—at
> least for others—while I was away from it. I have never
> seen thrushes' eggs of a blue equalling those we found
> there.
> No wonder Our Country was supernaturally
> beautiful. It had London for a foil and background;
> what is more, on that first day it wore an uncommon
> autumnal splendour, so that I cannot hope to meet
> again such heavily gilded elms smouldering in warm,
> windless sunshine, nor such bright meadows as they
> stood in, nor such blue sky and such white billowy
> cloud as rose up behind the oaks on its horizon.

In his poem, *And You, Helen*, among the gifts that he
would make to her is 'a clear eye, as good as mine'. Before
going on to see how clear and how good that was, we may
look at something he wrote in his *Richard Jefferies*, showing
how he valued the eye as more than a recorder:

> The clearness of the physical is allied to the penetration
> of the spiritual vision. For both are nourished to their
> perfect flowering by the habit of concentration. To see
> a thing as clearly as he saw the sun-painted yellow-
> hammer in Stewart's Mash is part of the office of the
> imagination. Imagination is no more than the making
> of graven images, whether of things on the earth or in
> the mind. To make them, clear concentrated sight and
> patient mind are the most necessary things after love;
> and these two are the children of love.

An intensity of enjoyment of 'The lovely visible earth and
sky and sea' is a spiritual enjoyment, it is disinterested in

being intense; and 'pure colour is rest of heart', as Jefferies wrote.

Thomas gave a good deal of thought to this question of seeing; later in the *Jefferies* there is this interesting analysis:

There are at least four ways of looking at visible things. Take, for example, a rough, thistly meadow at night.

One man sees a multitude of tall, pale thistles in a field of grey moonlight, knows them to be thistles, acknowledges the fact, and passes on without pause.

One is startled by their appearance. They are unlike thistles or any other plants as seen by day, and he has never seen them so before. He stops to make sure what they are, and at last remembers seeing them in a commonplace light by day, and he allows the first impression to die away.

Another sees them, and is startled, utterly forgetful that there was anything there when he passed before. He cannot reason about them, is too lazy or excited to go over and touch and see; he returns home with a tale of the unusual moonlight growth in the field at the edge of the wood. In an earlier age he might have reported the seeing of a mushroom flourishing of fairies.

Another sees them with a rapt placidity as something beautiful and new, and his recollection or discovery that they are thistles does not disturb his enjoyment. His eye and heart feed together upon their strangeness and beauty. He has really captured one of the visions which clear eyes and an untarnished soul are summoning continually from inexhaustible and eternal Nature.

Jefferies is often like the first, and the result of this kind of vision is his most pedestrian essay; at his best, as in 'The Pageant of Summer', he is like the last. . . .

From whatever position one looks at the prose, it is clear that Thomas brought in an exceptional degree, like Jefferies, the 'eye and heart' to feed on the 'strangeness and beauty' of the visible world. *The Woodland Life*, which is the work of a boy, is extraordinary for the number and the delicate accuracy of its first-hand observations. It was remarkable enough that a youth could and would quietly correct Gilbert White on certain points concerning sand-martins; and what might chiefly have suggested to a percipient reader that further development might be looked for, was the sustaining of the accuracy in the service of that particular bent and interest: the youth felt it worth while to attempt to describe the bloom on a sloe.

The world that has colour, that has light and shade, that shines, glows, glitters, that is dull, gloomy, dark, that sweeps, curves, juts out in crags, rises gently, falls in cliffs, that has an infinite number of things in it with those and kindred properties—the world, we might say in short, of the pictorial artist—was vividly present to Thomas; when expressing his perceptions of it, he does in fact often remind us of Jefferies. There is a painter's eye in this from the early *Horae Solitariae*:

> The shorn wheatfields in that mounded country were of a pale fluid yellow that mingled with the sky's blue, and was only here and there invaded by the lustrous green of an aftermath or the solid shadow of an immense elm; in it the little woods actually seemed to float.

And from the same book, the commonplace poetical manner of much of the following sentence doesn't cover over the delicacy of the perception at the end, a delicacy felt particularly in the union of 'twinkled' and 'silently':

> Full of joy we watched here the 'sweet and twenty' of perfect summer, when the matin shadows were once deleted, and the dew-globes evaporated from the hare-bell among the fern, or twinkled as they fell silently underfoot.

Light was a great beautifier for him: 'There was no substance to be seen that was not made precious', he says in *In Pursuit of Spring*, 'by the strong wind and the light

divine'; and in the same book: 'The soft bright gleam
with which the worn flagstones answered the returning
sun seemed to me pure Spring.' He is always fascinated by
the contiguity of bright and dark: 'In the sweet copses,
where the willow wren sings again in the highest branches,
the thorn foliage is so bright that the dark stems are
invisible' (*The Heart of England*). And the sort of colour
and light-and-shadow perceptiveness that reveals itself
when he is writing, in *Wales*, about a 'small unnecessary
pool' overhung by hazels, is richly in evidence in the
prose from first to last:

> In the summer, the surface was a lawn of duckweed on
> which the gloom from the hazels found something to
> please itself with, in a slow meditative way, by showing
> how green could grow from a pure emerald, at the edge
> of the shadow, into a brooding vapourish hue in the
> last recesses of the hazels.

It is not only the eye that is interested, quick, and sensitive. He knows, in autumn, 'the damp, cool crystal of the
air below the oaks and hazels of a lane'. He hears the gold-
crest repeating 'a tune like the unwinding of a tiny sweetly-
creaking winch, like the well-winch at home'. In the
Jefferies we have '. . . and in the still moist air before frost
the violet scent is expanding'. Mr Torrance, in *The
Happy-Go-Lucky Morgans*, speaks of 'smelling one of those
clusters of wild-carrot seeds, like tiny birds' nests, which
are scented like a ripe pear sweeter and juicier than ever
grew on pear-tree'.

Sometimes the perceptions have that surprising or
slightly odd quality that we call imaginative; things are
shown us in an aspect that is new and yet not arbitrary.
We recognize a true and vivid perception in his seeing the
thrushes standing 'with heads prouder than stags', and
mosses 'that were like moles of gilt and olive', and when

he says, 'The lightning grows upon the sky like a tumultu-
ous thorn tree of fire'. Occasionally the vision may seem
to be more fanciful than imaginative, as in 'the ash sprays
break up the low full moon into a flower of many sparks';
though in instances like this, where we may at first incline
to suspect hyperbole, it is best to reserve judgment at least
until we have been confronted with the same phenomena.
Sometimes there is certainly the possibility of our not fully
appreciating because we haven't the necessary 'specialist'
knowledge, as in 'And when the snowfall ceased with a
rush as upon the wings of a peregrine . . .'. That danger is
inherent, of course, in all nature writing, and great tact is
needed by the writer whose aims are not simply the
naturalist's. Most readers ought, one feels, to respond
pleasurably to the vividness and truth of the way in
which Thomas sees the peewits—those particular birds,
with crested head—as they settle, making the field 'all
a-flower by their alighting', and of his hearing the wood-
pigeons cooing 'with notes that were but as rounded
bubbles emerging from the silence and lost again'.

It has to be admitted that some of Thomas's prose
depends for its appeal on the reader's meeting it half-way
with a rather specialist interest. When he tells us that 'the
yew bark is plated and scaled and stained with greens and
reds and greys, powdered with green mould, and polished
in places to the colour of mahogany', we are given the
chance to see yew bark as we probably haven't yet seen it.
But for all that the writing is primarily informative and
is likely to be of interest to comparatively few people. The
specialist element in Thomas, however, is far too small to
be a danger to the interest of the 'general reader' of
nature writing. Even in these times most English people
would be familiar with a great deal of the material that he
is shaping into words.

Thomas had the gifts that would have enabled him to write nature books of an extraordinary sensuous lavishness. Indeed, some of the books—*The South Country, Wales, The Heart of England* are perhaps the chief of these—have such an abundance of enjoyed observations, such a power of apprehending certain aspects of nature, that we find ourselves thinking now of Keats, now of Jefferies. Thomas's sensuous endowment was like theirs. And yet he never achieved the sustained vigour and richness which they at their best achieved. There was, of course, his long-lasting inclination towards 'style', the style which often prevented or impeded the direct expression of sensuous actualities. Behind much of his 'fine writing' we can sense a capacity for original experience which we have to regret did not find a less ambiguous manner of expression. There is a chapter called 'Clouds over the Sea' (in *The Heart of England*), which makes us believe that Thomas saw clouds with a delicacy not surpassed even by Jefferies or by Hopkins in his remarkable prose notes. But the delicacy of eye and feeling is nearly lost among the hyperbole and eloquence. And yet it was not primarily a care for style, and not the reading of other authors, that ultimately impeded him from achieving his own rich expression of his sense of nature's fullness. There was a more deeply rooted tendency always at work. Before we go on to consider what this was, some excerpts will show what he did achieve in description.

Here is a passage from *The South Country*:

The colour of the dawn is lead and white—white snow falling out of a leaden sky to the white earth. The rose branches bend in sharper and sharper curves to the ground, the loaded yew sprays sweep the snow with white plumes. On the sedges the snow is in fleeces; the light strands of clematis are without motion, and have gathered it in clots. One thrush sings, but cannot long endure the sound of his unchallenged note; the sparrows chirrup in the ricks; the blackbird is waiting for the end of that low tingling noise of the snow falling straight in the windless air.

At mid-day the snow is finer, and almost rain, and it begins to pour down from its hives among the branches in short showers or in heavy hovering lumps. The leaves of ivy and holly are gradually exposed in all their gloomy polish, and out bursts the purple of the ash buds and the yellow of new foliage. The beech stems seem in their wetness to be made of a dark agate. Out from their tops blow rags of mist, and not far above them clouds like old spiders' webs go rapidly by.

For those who in their reading predominantly visualize and catch the aural references, there is a feast in Thomas's nature prose. But it is not often that he compels us with an unequivocal impression of strength, as Jefferies may at his best, and Keats, and, of course, Lawrence. The passage just given is characteristic of many in which we feel something of the effect of a notebook accumulation. The details are good, and the whole piece is in its way very impressive; few will care to feel superior in the presence of such an eye and such an interest. Nevertheless, the interest of the *writer*, as distinct from that of the nature observer, is rather too exclusively visual and aural. Reading these descriptions that have so many items in them, one sometimes has the impression that Thomas is being extremely conscientious and will leave nothing out; and sometimes the kind of items used and the manner of accumulating them in a description make us suspect that he has a certain number of words to write. Thinking in more general terms of a writer's progress and growth, and bearing in mind the amount of such writing that Thomas did, we may be likely to conclude that in piling up his

details of observation, first-hand and personally apprehended though they are, he is not writing out of his deepest
self and is in a sense holding back his development.

But those are large considerations; and with an eye on
what we actually have it is plain that the notebook habit
did not inevitably cramp him. The first chapter of *In
Pursuit of Spring* has many pages dealing with the weather
that preceded a certain March Easter (at which time he
was to start from London for the Quantocks), and the
writing there is spirited and vigorous. In the excerpt that
follows, the rhythm helps to give force to the records of his
sharp perceptiveness:

> There followed an ordinary fine day, warm but fresh,
> with more than one light shower out of the south-west
> during the afternoon; after that a cloudy, rainless day,
> which people did not call fine, though the chaffinches
> and thrushes enjoyed it wholly; and after that, rain
> again, and the elms standing about like conspirators in
> the mist of the rain, preparing something; then a day,
> warm and bright, of a heavenly and yet also a spirited
> loveliness—the best day of the year, when the larks'
> notes were far beyond counting; and after that wind
> and rain again; a day of great wind and no rain; then
> two days of mild, quick air, both glooming into black
> nights of tumult, with frosty, penitent-looking dawns.
> Snow succeeded, darkening the air, whitening the sky,
> on the wings of a strong wind from the north of north-
> west, for a minute only, but again and again, until by
> five o'clock the sky was all blue except at the horizon,
> where stood a cluster of white mountains, massive and
> almost motionless, in the south above the Downs, and
> round about them some dusky fragments not fit to be
> used in the composition of such mountains. They looked
> as if they were going to last for ever. Yet by six o'clock
> the horizon was dim, and the clouds all but passed
> away, the Downs clear and extended; the blackbird

singing as if the world were his nest, the wind cold and light, but dying utterly to make way for a beautiful evening of one star and many owls hooting.

Is there anyone in our literature who excels Thomas in quickness of response to seasonal atmospheres, to changes wrought in things by changing light, humidity, temperature? This interest of his is abundantly apparent from his first book onwards. Here is a passage from *The South Country*:

There are few things as pleasant as the thunder and lightning of May that comes in the late afternoon, when the air is as solid as the earth with stiff grey rain for an hour. There is no motion anywhere save of this perpendicular river, of the swaying rain-hit bough and quivering leaf. But through it all the thrushes sing, and jolly as their voices are the roars and echoes of the busy thunder quarrying the cliffs of heaven. And then the pleasure of being so wet that you may walk through streams and push through thickets and be none the wetter for it.

Before it is full night the light of the young moon falls for a moment out of a troubled but silent sky upon the young corn, and the tranquil bells are calling over the woods.

Then in the early morning the air is still and warm, but so moist that there is a soul of coolness in the heat, and never before were the leaves of the sorrel and wood sanicle and woodruff, and the grey-green foliage and pallid yellow flowers of the large celandine, so fair. The sudden wren's song is shrewd and sweet and banishes heaviness. The huge chestnut tree is flowering and full of bees. The parsley towers delicately in bloom. The beech boughs are encased in gliding crystal. The nettles, the millions of nettles in a bed, begin to smell of summer. In the calm and sweet air the turtle-doves murmur and the blackbirds sing—as if time were no more—over the mere.

EDWARD THOMAS

And the following is from the chapter 'August', in *The Heart of England*:

Nearer, and sometimes in the water, the branched meadow-sweet mingles the foam of its blossom and the profuse verdure of its leaves with willow herb, blue brook-lime, white cresses, and the dark purple figwort. A mellow red, like that of autumn oaks or hawthorn at the first touch of spring, tinges the meadow-sweet. The disposition of its flowers is so exquisite that they seem to have been moulded to the shape of some delicate hand; every bud takes part in the effect. The lithe meanders of the stems are contrasted with the intricacy of the goose-grass and the contortion of the forget-me-nots. Both in the midst of the long stalk and in the plume of flowers the branching is so fine and the curves rely so intimately upon one another that a simple copy on paper is cool and pensive after the vanity of cultivated curiousness. Hardly anywhere is there a visible shadow; at most there is a strange tempering of pure light that throws a delicate bloom upon the cattle and the birds, and a kind of seriousness upon the face or flower within its influence. A dark insect of clear wings alights upon the new hawkweed flower, and sits probing deliciously in its deep heart; but, although the petals are in the midst of grasses and under thorns, the fly perches unshadowed, and throws no shade beyond a moistening of the flower's gold. The close purple flowers of the vetches are scarcely duller in the recesses, where the plant begins to climb, than at the summit where the buds bear a fine down. The fish gleam deep in the pool. The dark ivy shines in the innermost parts of the wood.

Finally, in this endeavour to suggest what the essentials are in Thomas's sensibility as shown in his response to the 'sensuous abundance' element of the natural world, here is an excerpt from *Wales*:

The last village was far behind. The last happy chapel-
goer had passed me long ago. A cock crowed once and
said the last word on repose. The rain fell gently; the
stems of the hazels in the thickets gleamed; and the
acorns in the grassy roads, and under the groups of oaks,
showed all their colours, and especially the rosy hues
where they had but just before been covered by the cup.
One by one I saw the things which make the autumn
hedges so glorious and strange at a little distance: the
yellow ash trees, with some green leaves; the hoary and
yellow willows; the hawthorns, purple and crimson and
green; the briars, with most hips where there were few-
est leaves; the green brambles with red fruit and black;
tall, grey, and leafless thistles with a few small crimson
flowers; the grey-green nettles with purple stems; the
ragwort flowers; and on the long, green, wet grass the
fallen leaves shining under red and yellow oaks; and
through the olive lances of hazel the fields shining in
patines of emerald. Doves cooed in the oaks, pheasants
gleamed below. The air was full of the sweetness of the
taste of blackberries, and the scent of mushrooms and
of crumbling wild-carrot seeds, and the colour of the
yellow, evening grass. The birches up on the hills above
were golden, and like flowers. Between me and them a
smouldering fire once or twice sent up dancing crimson
flames, and the colour and perfume of the fire added
themselves to the power of the calm, vast, and windless
evening, of which the things I saw were as a few shells
and anemones at the edge of a great sea. The valley
waited and waited.

These extracts—they are representative even in what
might at first seem to be incidental elements, for instance
the presence of rain and wet—are obviously not just a
naturalist's writing. What they give is less the sense of a
record of items observed than of keen enjoyment. Not that
the writing is always swift and to the mark; there are con-
ventionalities and commonplaces: 'the disposition of its

flowers', 'profuse verdure', 'There are few things more pleasant', 'as if time were no more'. But the total effect isn't commonplace. For one thing there is a certain integrity simply in the *care* with which so much detail is provided; the writing is not the result—to use his own interesting phrase—of 'the vanity of cultivated curiousness'. Then there is a sensuous freshness going with an emphasis on things most delicately perceived: the fly that 'throws no shade beyond a moistening of the flower's gold', the exquisite branching of the stem and flowers of the meadow-sweet. But most significant for us is a presence which, while it doesn't neutralize the 'keen' of the phrase used above, suggests that 'a sense of keen enjoyment' is far too simple an account of what is conveyed. I am not thinking of the north winds, the leaden skies, the 'black nights of tumult'; but of 'the elms standing about like conspirators in the mist, preparing something', of the meadow-sweet tinged with 'a mellow red, like that of autumn oaks or hawthorn at the first touch of spring', of the dark ivy that 'shines in the innermost parts of the wood', of the wren's song that is 'shrewd and sweet and banishes heaviness', and of the last lines of the *Wales* excerpt; and of rain, and light and shadow, and sound and silence. The presence is not always strongly felt, but it is always there. Sometimes it is stressed by Thomas in a cliché like 'as if time were no more', and sometimes in a hinting at a profundity and a strangeness as in 'A cock crowed once and said the last word on repose', and 'the things I saw were as a few shells and anemones at the edge of a great sea'. But mostly it is contained in the description itself. For the moment we can call the presence a sense of change and transience; later we shall know it for something more complex than that, something not definable simply in those terms. Such a sense was too strong in

Thomas to let him feel anything like security even in the contemplation of autumn's fullness. To feel autumn characteristically as the end of summer and the beginning of winter is as valid a way of feeling as any other. But the expression in writing of such a response, while by no means precluded from sensuous richness, is not likely to be characterized by vigour and power.

The use of a word like 'joy', as of 'happiness', is a delicate matter; but while it may be true that Thomas, so finely endowed for enjoyment, never felt free fully to enjoy (not, however, that he is to be 'explained' as a frustrated hedonist), it is clear that his joy in nature was profound and was not diminished but refined by that subtle sense and thought of transience. However we may interpret 'joy', it is a fact that Thomas in his prose never ceased to advocate, in ways varying between the logical-detached and the lyrical-fervid, enjoyment of nature as an end. He frequently quotes Jefferies' passages describing an ecstatic delight in sky, sun, sea, flowers, leaves, trees. It is the 'joy' in Jefferies that he emphasizes as most valuable in him: 'No man could be neglected', Thomas writes, 'who had so much knowledge which it is impossible to acquire by effort and time alone; his power of showing the joy in things, and of making them a means to joy, gives him still higher claims'; he says that not to have heard the brook amid all the sadness of *The Story of My Heart* 'is to have missed the joyous heart of the work'; and while seeing that some of the eloquence there 'is the hectic flush of the man doomed to an early death', he speaks—with Blake perhaps in the background—of 'the holiness of its [the book's] energy'.

Thomas himself often expounds something of a nature philosophy, stressing a sense of blessedness to be gained in the contact with nature, and expressing a hope and

65

sometimes even a belief in mankind's regeneration by such contact. When he writes out these ideas and the feelings from which they seemingly rise, he is as often as not verbose. 'The Stile', from *Light and Twilight*, gives an interesting account of his thoughts and feelings at the end of a day spent walking with a friend, a day marked by the gradual coming-on of an 'ease and confidence'; but the sense of a joy-bringing at-oneness, which at the conclusion of the essay he claims to have experienced, is stated rather than undeniably *there*. Here is the concluding page of the essay (he is going home alone at evening):

> I did not disturb the dark rest and beauty of the earth which had ceased to be ponderous, hard matter and had become itself cloudy or, as it is when the mind thinks of it, spiritual stuff, so that the glow-worms shone through it as stars through clouds. I found myself running without weariness or heaviness of the limbs through the soaked overhanging grass. I knew that I was more than the something which had been looking out all that day upon the visible earth and thinking and speaking and tasting friendship. Somewhere—close at hand in that rosy thicket or far off beyond the ribs of sunset—I was gathered up with an immortal company, where I and poet and lover and flower and cloud and star were equals, as all the little leaves were equal ruffling before the gusts, or sleeping and carved out of the silentness. And in that company I had learned that I am something which no fortune can touch, whether I be soon to die or long years away. Things will happen which will trample and pierce, but I shall go on, something that is here and there like the wind, something unconquerable, something not to be separated from the dark earth and the light sky, a strong citizen of infinity and eternity. The confidence and ease had become a deep joy; I knew that I could not do without the Infinite, nor the Infinite without me.

The philosophy there, given such an eloquent exposition, may seem to be more willed than profoundly motivated; we are not strongly compelled, as we ought to be in a matter of such claimed significance; there is rather too much mere assertion. But clearly there is behind the writing some experience that had been of value to, as well as valued by, Thomas, and as clearly there was something in him that wanted passionately to believe in the possibility of such a consummation.

His 'doctrine' of a possible blessedness to be achieved even if only momentarily, owes something, of course, to Wordsworth. Poems like 'It is the first mild day of March', and 'Expostulation and Reply', and 'The Tables Turned', could easily be related to this:

> But it was one of those days when what meets the eye is far less than what is apprehended, when a man may spend all the hours of light out of doors and see nothing and hear nothing and yet be profoundly blessed. The birds, the trees, the houses, the few flowers, may indeed be seen, and the songs heard from branch and sky, but all these little things are dwarfed, and, in the memory, sometimes quite shut out by the sense of the presence of earth itself, the huge, quiet, all-sustaining earth mutely communing with the sun. (From the essay 'Winter Music', in *Light and Twilight*)

And when Thomas writes (in *The Country*, which is a little hodge-podge of interesting thinking, philosophy, description, anthologizing, literary criticism, fantasy), the following:

> We may feel the painful splendour of our humanity in the town, but it is in the country more often that we become aware, in a sort of majestic quiet, of the destiny which binds us to infinity and eternity,

we shall probably think of *The Prelude*, perhaps even of specific lines:

Our destiny, our being's heart and home
Are with infinitude, and only there.

But to say that an English nature-writer is indebted to
Wordsworth is to say little or nothing. He is here men-
tioned only as one of the more obvious 'inspirations' of
Thomas's explicit nature-philosophizing.

That 'Nature never did betray The heart that loved
her' is a belief-statement capable of various responses and
interpretations, from the loosely emotional to the strictly
logical. Thomas, at any rate, frequently writes of nature
as a beneficent and educative force. His tendency to create
young people, especially women, who owe their perfection
to a nature environment, has already been mentioned as
at least in part deriving from 'Lucy' and from certain of
the heroines of Jefferies. He dwells glowingly and at
great length on Félise, the child of Nature in *The Dewy
Morn* (though he has reservations about some of Jefferies'
claims for her). Time and again he quotes from Jefferies
sentences like this: 'These breadths [of sea and sky] draw
out the soul; we feel that we have wider thoughts than we
know; the soul has been living, as it were, in a nutshell,
all unaware of its own power, and now suddenly finds
freedom in the sun and sky.' He writes of Jefferies: 'He
wished to plunge human thought into sea and air and
green things that it might be restored.' There were, of
course, times when he felt that such a restoration was a
romantic hope, but he never tired of imagining a perfection: of the effect of a thrush's song on the 'Other Man',
in *In Pursuit of Spring*, he says: '. . . it made him think he
would gladly live no longer than a thrush if he could do
some one thing as right, as crisp and rich, as the song was'.
But while he endorses the desire for such a perfection, his
caution imposes that half-dubious 'it made him think . . .'

Thomas has passages whose whole tendency and tone

suggest the more exalted element in Jefferies; there is this, for instance, from the chapter entitled 'The Pride of the Morning', in *The Heart of England*:

> But the sky is of an eager, luminous pale blue that speaks of health and impetuousness and success. Across it, low down, lie pure white clouds, preserving, though motionless, many torn and tumultuous forms; they have sharp edges against the blue and invade it with daggers of the same white; they are as vivid in their place in that eager sky as yews on a pale, bright lawn, or as lightning in blue night. If pure and hale intelligence could be visibly expressed, it would be like that. The eyes of the wayfarer at once either dilate in an effort for a moment at least to be equal in beauty with the white and blue, clear sky, or they grow dim with dejection at the impossibility. The brain also dilates and takes deep breaths of life, and casts out stale thought and coddled emotion. It scorns afterthought as the winds are flouting the penitent dawn.

Writing like this clearly has affinities with the Jefferies adumbrated in the preceding paragraph. The kind of wider life that it posits, and the effect on the 'brain', as on the 'eyes', of the sky's colour and forms, recall Jefferies. In the second half of the extract the formality towards which the declarations tend does not destroy the force that this particular ideal has for Thomas; the expressed dislike of 'stale thought and coddled emotion' is not perfunctory.

There is a lapse occasionally into what I think may be fairly called a manufactured mystical attitude, as in some of the utterances of Arthur Bishopstone the outcast, the unfortunate, in *The Icknield Way*: in the barn in winter, 'it is cold, yes, but the frost is one of the angels', and out of this barn, says an entry in the outcast's notebook, may come a flame, a prayer, a rose of regeneration for the world. The concern behind the writing is real, but the sincerity is imperfect because thought has not been clear and precise enough.

Often, however, the beliefs and claims are less transcendental, and are likely to be the more life-enhancing for being more substantial. It is a fact that the line of the Downs can be, as he says it is, both strengthening and calming. The mole-catcher can really have 'the sharpness of sense and economy of words that bespeak a healthy mind cleansed by the pure hillside air'; though such men are much rarer now than when those words were written (in *The Woodland Life*) nearly sixty years ago. Nature can valuably quieten; Thomas's experience when he writes in *The Last Sheaf* of the historic Dark Lane of the Pilgrim's Way to St. David's, is by no means singular (except perhaps in certain details of knowledge):

> I had no conscious thought of antiquity, or of anything older than the wet green money-wort leaves on the stone of the banks beside me, or the points of gorse blossom, or a jackdaw's laughter in the keen air. If the pilgrims never entered my mind, neither did living people. The lane itself, just for what it was, absorbed and quieted me.

He can write coolly and clearly about enjoyment of nature, as here, from *The South Country*:

> Sea, mountains, 'bad weather', inconvenient solitude, are unlikely to be much admired until the man who is to admire them is free from fear and in every way practically safe from them,

and about nature study for schools:

> Pursued out of doors where those creatures, moving and still, have their life and their beauty, knowledge is real. The senses are invited there to the subtlest and most

delightful training, and have before them an immeasurable fresh field. . . . Let us also be careful to have knowledge as well as enthusiasm in our masters. Enthusiasm alone is not enthusiasm.

The same coolness and good sense are in evidence when he is writing on a theme that could have easily lent itself to the expression of airy nothings:

> Blake relates the flower to Eternity. Calming us with its space and patience, the country relates us all to Eternity. We go to it as would-be poets, or as solitaries, vagabonds, lovers, to escape foul air, noise, hard hats, black uniforms, multitudes, confusion, incompleteness, elaborate means without clear ends—to escape ourselves; and we do more than escape them. So vastly do we increase the circle of which we are the centre that we become as nothing. The larger the circle the less seems our distance from other men each at his separate centre; and at last that distance is nothing at all in the mighty circle, and all have but one circumference. And thus we truly find ourselves. Many cannot bear this expanding circle, this devouring silence, and they seek another kind of nearness by crowding to Eastbourne or the Bay of Naples, but do not succeed entirely in evading the greatness of sun, wind, and sea.

It is clear that the ideas and beliefs given in this steady writing, whatever we may feel as to their derivation from previous thinkers, are firmly held. Moreover, the passage, despite its being tinged with a personal metaphysic—'this devouring silence'—seems to me to hint at valuable truths about certain aspects of the relations between men and of men's relation to 'Eternity'. Thomas did not, of course, go very far with that kind of exploration; 'hint at' is a fair measure of the distance.

Edward Thomas, then, had the kind of perceptiveness which can bring 'joy' from contact with the sensuous world of nature. And he was richly and wonderfully acquainted with that world. Moreover, he often expressed the doctrine of the value of joy, and was not infrequently one of the 'preachers loud in the land' that he refers to in *The Country*. One of his most exhilarating descriptions—it is not often that we find ourselves using that epithet for him—is in the chapter 'January Sunshine', from *The Heart of England*. It is too lengthy to give in its entirety, but its character and tone can be suggested fairly enough for our purpose by summary and by selected quotation. It has, under the January sun, shining grass, glowing rusty oaks and farm roofs, bare clean glittering hedges, 'blackthorn ruddy where the cattle have rubbed', a skylark and linnets scattering song, 'immense crystal spaces of fine windy air' in which jackdaws soar, float, dance, dive, cry. Brass furnishings of the horses gleam, their tails stream out, the plough is silvery. 'A pheasant is hurled out of a neighbouring copse', and a fox crosses the road and the meadow, 'tall and red, going easily as if he sailed in the wind'. The hounds appear: 'Run hard, hounds'; and then, 'Run hard, fox, and may you escape, for it would not be well to die on such a day'. May it escape the 'foolish ones who now break through the hedge on great horses . . . ignorant of the command that has gone forth from the heart of this high blue heaven, Be beautiful and enjoy and live'. That is the essence of the chapter, and whatever our response may be to the writing and the message of the last line or two, after-events and especially the manner of his death give a touch of pathos and a sufficiently bitter irony to that 'Be beautiful and enjoy and live' which came from 'the heart of this high blue heaven'. But in any case there were qualities in Thomas which made his gospel impossible of fulfilment for himself. The more than usually sharp sense of transience has already been touched upon. There was also his peculiar awareness of 'unknown modes of being', an awareness which in fact is likely to recall the 'huge peak, black and huge' that made Wordsworth's brain

> Work with a dim and undetermined sense
> Of unknown modes of being; o'er my thoughts
> There hung a darkness, call it solitude
> Or blank desertion.

By examining that awareness in Thomas we shall see how much more than a pressing sense of transience it was that went towards making his apprehension of life subtle and so delicately poised between—to put it simply for the moment—joy and sadness, hope and despair. And there are, of course, other factors to be considered not specifically connected with response to nature.

Thomas's sense of 'otherness' in nature, that quality or aspect which in its independence and utter apartness from human life makes a strange and often powerful and disturbing impact on the *human* mind, was deep and lifelong. It had profound implications for his life, character, and writing.

In the early writing particularly, the awareness of the 'mysterious other' tends to be referred to, rather than powerfully realized. Often the reference is formal, as here in *Horae Solitariae*:

> I cannot walk under trees without a vague powerful feeling of reverence. Calmly persuasive, they ask me to bow my head to the unknown god. In the evening, especially, when the main vocation of sight is to suggest what eyes cannot see, the spacious and fragrant shadow of oak or pine is a temple which seems to contain the very power for whose worship it is spread.

The mystery is only thinly there, explicitly claimed rather

than evoked. Similarly with the following, from the same book:

> But the silence was mysteriously great, because the incalculably subtle sound of the ocean was ever there, solemnizing, deepening, and as it were charging with 'large utterance' the silence it could not break.

Nevertheless, the big words and gestures do not altogether hide a reaching-out towards an interesting way of experiencing. And in a passage like this from *The Heart of England*, where he is writing about a solitary dying ash tree at the edge of a pond, it is clearly anything but a common mind that is at work:

> I have approached it on some moonlit midnights, when the sky was so deep that the tall oaks were as weeds at the bottom of an unfathomed sea, and it has stood up erect and puissant, as if it were the dreamer at one with all he sees, in a world of blind men with open eyes.

In spite of the tendency to explain at too great length the feeling of the mystery, and thereby dissipating its power, there are many places in Thomas where we are made to feel something of the strangeness. In the last essay of *Cloud Castle*, entitled 'The Moon', he tells how, not being able to sleep indoors, he goes out into the night. He describes sky and moon, and earth 'with lakes of moonblaze on the plains and mists of moonlit chalk on the hills amid the blackness'. In the dark wood he sees light on the trunk of a tree, one tree only; it is the moonlight playing alone, without spectators: 'I was a pure accident.' There is a sort of gaiety about the play, but ultimately solemnity has the upper hand: 'This was the kind of play that makes the frost flowers on dead sticks in the woods on winter nights.' It does not amuse him any more than the majesty of the moon amuses him:

I buried myself in a haycock not far from the trees and
fell asleep thinking that the sky was a pool strewn with
swansdown along the currents. The wash of waves
among the reeds at the edge of the land was, I suppose,
the unceasing rhythmless sound of wind in the trees. I
awoke several times in the face of the same white moon
and immense woods, seething always in the light continuous wind.

So the short essay ends. The force of the original experience is, I think, weakened by touches of analysis and
explanation of the non-vital kind, but in many places we
do feel, through the direct language, the strength of the
writer's feeling of strangeness, of otherness.

The consciousness of this particular aspect of nature is,
of course, felt in many modern writers; in varying degrees
of significance, of intensity and persistence, it is in Conrad,
Lawrence, L. H. Myers; E. M. Forster and T. S. Eliot
recognize its force even if they do not often present it with
strong immediacy. In none of these writers is it more
persistent than in Thomas, in none of them is it a bigger
and more integral part of the whole consciousness.

Fear, and awe, and reverence of the 'other', can join to
make a response of great power. Such a response may, of
course, become the root from which springs a whole view
of life, a philosophy, a religion. Exaltation, too, may be an
effect of this disturbing intercourse of man and nature.
Wordsworth, it will be remembered, gave thanks to the
'Wisdom and Spirit of the Universe' for the 'severer
interventions' employed by nature (together with her
'fearless visitings'), and for the

> . . . dark
> Inscrutable workmanship that reconciles
> Discordant elements.

He states that he was given such an understanding as made
him recognize 'A grandeur in the beatings of the heart'.

Edward Thomas's gratitude to life was of a different kind and found different expression. It is as true of him as of Wordsworth that he was 'Fostered alike by beauty and by fear'. But with him, while the love of beauty lasted and grew, the 'fear' did not help to form any positive faith: 'the intimations are not of immortality', says F. R. Leavis in *New Bearings in English Poetry*. In passing, it may be interesting to note that whereas Wordsworth's early profound faith, the faith that enabled him to write some great poetry, changed and dried into something less personal and more conventional, the man with no semblance of a 'belief' grew into the kind of personal and radical understanding without which there can be no true creativity.

Some of the objects and motives of Thomas's sense of what we call in general 'fear' are given explicitly in the prose. There is the loneliness he felt when a vast London silence took hold of him:

> A puissant spell it was; by some means more subtle and direct than thought, I realized my own intense loneliness. Then the very rain falling patiently had a magic hold on me, and I stopped my ears as if a Siren sang. (*Cloud Castle*)

That is obviously very early writing—how fond he was of 'puissant'—but the theme is wholly characteristic. Then there is a feeling of the cold power of water:

> The river ran by, grim, dark, and vast, and having been untouched by history, old as hills and stars. . . . How tameless and cold the water, alien, careless, monstrous, capable of drowning in a little while the uttermost agony or joy and making them as if they had never been. (*The Heart of England*)

And of the cold silent air:

> . . . or when the cold and entirely silent air under a purple November sky chills the blood, so that friend-

ship and hopes and purposes are all in vain as in an opiate dream. (*The Heart of England*)

An immense, empty marshland mingles itself with the grey sea, and he says:

> All that greyness takes hold upon the mind like autumn rain and lures it to we know not what desperate carelessness. (*The Heart of England*)

In the same book, the evening light shines on some water in a wood:

> But as I walked and the wind fell for the sunset, the path led me under high, stony beeches. The air was cool and still and moist and waterish dark, and no bird sang. A wood-pigeon spread out his barry tail as he ascended perpendicularly to a hidden place among the branches, and then there was no sound. The waterish half-light seemed to have lasted for ever and to have an eternity ahead. Through the trees a grassy, deeply-rutted road wound downwards, and at the edge the ruts were broad and full of dark water. Still retaining some corruption of the light of the day upon its surface, that shadowed water gave an immense melancholy to the wood. The reflections of the beeches across it were as the bars of a cage that imprisoned some child of light. It was but a few inches deep of rain, and yet, had it been a legendary pool, or had a drowned woman's hair been stamped into the mud at its edge and left a green forehead exposed, it could not have stained and filled the air more tragically. The cold, the silence, the leaflessness found an expression in that clouded shining surface among the ruts.

When he describes, in *Wales*, a lake in wild Welsh country, he likes to think of the legend connected with it rather than of the lake itself:

> ... for when I see the water for ever waved except among the weeds in the centre, and see the water-lily leaves

lifted and resembling a flock of wild-fowl, I cannot always be content to see it so remote, so entirely inhuman.

Worth noting at this point is the way in which, right from the beginning of Thomas's writing, small vulnerable things are often seen against a vast background, and sounds heard against the great silence. In his first book, 'Under a blackening sky a solitary heron goes over in silence', and we hear 'the challenge of the blue-tits in the dense firs'.

Fear, melancholy uneasiness, solemnity are not, however, the inevitable effect for Thomas of such scenes and situations and happenings. Those feelings are there in the prose abundantly; not always powerfully there, and often half-hidden in over-writing, they are nevertheless there consistently enough to impress us with their essential part in his mind and temperament. But what at one time may darken or 'terrify' him, at another calms, is beautiful, strengthens. Of a certain area not far from the Ridgeway in Wiltshire he writes:

> A fair land is this on a still, rainy and misty winter day, with its wide unoccupied fields and dreaming trees— no men, no sound, and the Downs as imaginary as the sea-noise in a shell. (*Richard Jefferies*)

Bird-song is not inevitably for him an ineffectual challenge to the abyss of silence; the song itself is accepted sometimes as an illuminating voice of otherness, as in *The South Country*, where after a description of the nightingale's song, a description which puts the emphasis on the impetuosity, the liquid sweetness, and the wild purity, he comments:

> Beautiful as the notes are for their quality and order, it is their inhumanity that gives them their utmost fascina-

tion, the mysterious sense which they bear to us that the earth is something more than a human estate, that there are things not human yet of great power and honour in the world.

Loneliness and storm are not inevitably frightening; and David Morgan, the misfit—one of the misfits—of *The Happy-Go-Lucky Morgans*, who being dissatisfied with civilization builds a tower in the mountains and hopes to create out of his contemplation of nature a new religion for men, speaks for a 'mood' of Thomas when he says:

> I am alone. From my tower I look out at the huge desolate heaves of the grey beacons. Their magnitude and pure form give me a great calm. . . . The sheer mountains, on some days, seem to be the creation of my own lean terrible thoughts, and I am glad: the soft, wooded hills below and behind seem the creation of the pampered luxurious thought which I have left in the world of many men.

And when Morgan dies, during a night of great storm, the narrator on the following morning, which is quiet, is still aware of the storm somewhere in his mind, and it is to the storm's fury that he attributes the present great calm and beauty; walking in the quiet coomb he recalls the night's happenings, and after giving a vivid impression of the storm he says:

> I looked out from the death room, having turned away from the helpless, tranquil bed and the still wife, and saw the hillside trees surging under a wild moon, but they were strange and no longer to be recognized, while the earth was heaving and be-nightmared by the storm. It was the awe of that hour which still hung over the coomb, making its clearness so solemn, its silence so pregnant, its gentleness so sublime. How fresh it was after the sick room, how calm after the vain conflict with death.

But the allusions, numerous though they are, to a sustenance to be drawn from the otherness of nature, do little to dispel our main impression that otherness is predominantly disturbing to Thomas, disturbing in that it has a quiet power to deepen his brooding reflective tendency. It is not the kind of disturbance that brings about protests against the cruelty or heartlessness of nature; intense cold, for instance, is not to Thomas a destroying force in the way that it is to Hardy: he does not see it as a killer of birds, though no one ever was quicker than he to see a bird so killed and to feel what he saw. It is the very existence of 'other' phenomena that moves him deep within, and he can never exactly explain why. A characteristic description is this from *The Heart of England*:

On one side, for some miles, ran a large fell that was a home and playground for winds, steep and long to be crossed, and all white and grim, shutting out home and the pleasures that are found among men. On the other side, steep also and wildly shaped with small, precipitous crags and angry surf of heather and here and there haggish thorns, lay a moor. Between these two the road rose and fell over lesser but steep hills, and from one hilltop I could see the sea beyond the moor. It was grey, without light, with long quivering lines that never ended, but insubstantial; it seemed rather the grisly offspring of a mind made pregnant by the wintry melancholy. The mountains came down to the edge of it, like lions to drink, ten miles away. Not a house was visible, and on the sea the few ships were like the water itself, inventions of my own, as it were, which I had launched upon that infinite desolation for sport.

All day, ahead and always at the same distance, rose high mountains, with crude outlines as of heavy and frosty land fresh turned by the plough; the long ravines of snow upon their sides made their peaks more sharp and their heights more sudden. They haunted the day.

This description, with its emphasis on crude shape, sudden steeps, greyness and whiteness, magnitude, distances, is vivid enough to impress us with the justice of those four last words: the mountains were there all the time at the back of the day, and they were an intrusion upon his daylight consciousness. (It is not merely the word 'mountains' that prompts the suggestion that Thomas would have profoundly understood Hopkins's

> O the mind, mind has mountains, cliffs of fall
> Frightful, sheer, no-man-fathomed.)

Then a little later we have this:

And there still were the mountains ahead. Their painful distances of long, white, houseless steeps made the mind suffer the body's agony of toiling there, of being lost there in storm, of being there on a still, dark night. They bred—by means of natural, human sympathy with the difficulty of life among such heights, by the horror of the distance, the coldness, the whiteness—a languor out of which emerged infinite admiration and awe, a sense of beauty even, and unquestionably a kind of pride in the powers of the human spirit that can dwell upon the earth and be the equal of these things, sharing with them the sunlight and the darkness, enduring like them vicissitudes, decay, violent disaster, and like them disbelieving in the future and in death, except for others.

The rhetoric into which the writing has passed suggests that the sustaining thoughts which he says the mountains have inspired in him are more willed than actual. The kind of assertiveness represented by 'unquestionably a kind of pride in the powers of the human spirit . . .' is both stereotyped and inflated; in fact, thought and diction are largely cliché in that last long sentence. The recurrence of commonplace phrases like 'sharing with them the sunlight and the darkness' reveals the sort of relaxation which comes from an incompleteness of sincerity. If he had had a profound interest in what he was saying, he would not have made those stale yet futile comparisons between men and mountains. He may have felt 'infinite admiration and awe', but we are conscious here of big words only, and the 'even' of 'a sense of beauty even' shows an uncertainty and the phrase has anything but a positive force. The three last words of the passage, though true enough as an indication of a way in which we tend to think, introduce a note that is jarring in its rather obvious irony, and which in fact quarrels with the 'optimism' of the preceding lines. When he continues his description of the hills at nightfall, he sees them as 'purely beautiful, while over them a large, simple sunset threw a golden bridge between towering, white, still clouds'. But it was not the effect of the 'large, simple sunset' (vague phrase, saying little), nor the thoughts of men's spiritual triumphs, that Thomas recalled with his profoundest feeling, but that sea 'grey, and without light', and the mountains that 'haunted the day'.

Mountains, then, had for Edward Thomas a symbolic force or value quite different from their value as an incitement to thoughts of men's heroic qualities. The cold, the vastness, the bareness, the silence, emphasized his loneliness. To speak thus may be simplifying what is a very subtle matter; yet it is clear that a feeling of loneliness is at the root of much of Thomas's thought and writing. In *Wales*, following a day on which he had seen a company of oaks made glorious by a sudden sunlight in January but had not been able to imagine himself among them—'They were holding festival, but not for me'—he is again among the mountains:

All day I wandered over an immense, bare, snowy mountain which had looked as round as a white summer cloud, but was truly so pitted and scarred and shattered by beds of streams and valleys full of rotten oak trees, that my course wound like a river's or like a mouse's in a dense hedge. The streams were small, and, partly frozen, partly covered up by snow, they made no noise. Nothing made any noise. There was a chimney stack clearly visible ten miles away, and I wished that I could hear the factory hiss and groan. No wind stirred among the trees. Once a kite flew over among the clouds of the colour of young swans' plumage, but silently, silently. I passed the remains of twelve ancient oaks, like a litter of some uncouth, vast monster pasturing, but without a sound.

He describes a ruined farm, and implements, and naked trees. He thinks of the inns of his journey: 'How could their fires have survived the all-pervading silent snow?' As he walks farther and farther, the extent of the hills ahead and around becomes greater, the cold persists, he imagines more and more distances. And then suddenly there is red in the sky: 'I knew that red: it belonged to the old world: it was the colour of the oast houses in Kent.' He sees a light, hears a bell, finds himself among sheep, hears a stream again, and thinks of Borrow: 'Borrow, I remembered, knew the stream. Borrow! I was at home again.'

The thought-feeling beneath this dichotomy—here the cold, the silence, the immensity, there the inn, fires, company—is one of the strongest things in Thomas's temperament and sensibility, and one of the chief determinants of his 'view of life'. The feeling is, of course, common enough, even universal, in a simple form; but the difference, the great difference, between Thomas and the man who is glad of fire and company is that he goes beyond gladness at comfort, while welcoming it, and is acutely conscious of what the fire is symbolical of, and that he feels intensely the power of the 'other', the power which is neutralized perhaps, for a time, by the fire. He had this way of thinking and feeling from an early age: in *Wales*, he recalls a holiday spent when a boy, when there were large red apples, and smoked salmon and hams perfuming the kitchen, and shining candlesticks, and crisp and wavy oaten bread to be eaten with buttermilk,

> . . . and the great fire shook his rustling sheaf of flames and laughed at the wind and rain that stung the window-panes; and sometimes a sense of triumph arose from the glory of the fire and the vanity of the wind, and sometimes a sense of fear lest the fire should be conspiring with the storm.

Thomas is likely to remind us of Conrad and his sense of a silent immensity finally absorbing things seen and heard and men's thoughts and activities. Conrad repeatedly gives explicit utterance to this sense, or this thought, sometimes with great impressiveness and sometimes more or less perfunctorily. It is, of course, most impressive when it is an organic part of the whole work, part of the whole vision, throwing into relief and being a comment upon the vanity of men, or the greed, or the lust and pride, or the mistaken idealism, or the loyalty, the courage, the endurance: in works like *Nostromo*, *Heart of Darkness*, *Typhoon*, mountains and sky and sea, the jungle, the wind, are part of the whole pattern and organization. Thomas must have felt very deeply the force of writing like that at the end of *Nostromo*, when Linda's last great cry of 'Gian Battista!' travels over the waters of the Placid Gulf:

> Dr Monygham, pulling round in the police-galley, heard the name pass over his head. It was another of Nostromo's triumphs, the greatest, the most enviable,

the most sinister of all. In that true cry of undying passion that seemed to ring aloud from Punta Mala to Azuera and away to the bright line of the horizon, overhung by a big white cloud shining like a mass of solid silver, the genius of the magnificent Capataz de Cargadores dominated the dark gulf containing his conquests of treasure and love.

And he must have responded sharply to the feeling that lies behind the account of the onset of the storm in *Typhoon*:

> It was something formidable and swift, like the sudden smashing of a vial of wrath. It seemed to explode all round the ship with an overpowering concussion and a rush of great waters, as if an immense dam had been blown up to windward. In an instant the men lost touch of each other. This is the disintegrating power of a great wind: it isolates one from one's kind. . . . A furious gale attacks him like a personal enemy, tries to grasp his limbs, fastens upon his mind, seeks to rout his very spirit out of him.

One would not wish to develop at length any comparison between Conrad and Thomas, despite this striking similarity in their consciousness of the 'dark gulf' (Conrad's phrase), 'the immense dark force' (Thomas's phrase). The fundamental difference between them is perhaps that Conrad, in dominating his knowledge of the 'gulf' (as the 'cry of undying passion' gave Nostromo a kind of victory over it), could turn to the world of human endeavour and thought and find there matter for an art which has its dark side in the presentment of human weaknesses and evil, but which is not gloomily pessimistic because it has the strength of significant and penetrating recognitions. Neither is the art of Thomas—his poetry—gloomy; he, too, finds nourishment in life, as we have seen and shall see. But the art is a smaller thing than Conrad's mainly because it is more personal; it is a matter mostly of Thomas himself and what he feels and thinks in his world, and he does not escape into a wider contemplation of human life. But it will help us if we remind ourselves that his world is a narrow one only by comparison with that of the great writers, and that his world is our own world to a much larger extent than we may have recognized or that we may care fully to recognize.

That dichotomy so central in Thomas, of cold vastness and near warmth, of solitude and company, and so on, has an interesting parallel—I cannot say whether it is cause or effect—in a way he has of seeing 'the near and the far' and of feeling something significant in their presence together. Passages like the following are frequent in the prose; it is from *Wales*, and he is again speaking of hills towards which he is walking as the sun begins to rise behind him:

> Before, a range of hills stood up against the cold sky with bold lines such as a happy child will draw who has much paper and a stout crayon, and looked so that I remembered the proverb which says, that if a man goes up Cader Idris at night, by dawn he is dead, or mad, or a poet. They were immense; they filled half the sky; yet in the soft light that felt its way glimmeringly, and as if fearfully, among their vast valleys and along their high crags, they looked like ruins of something far more mighty; the fields also, on this side of them, and all the alder-loving streams and massy woods, were but as the embers of something which the night had made and had only half destroyed before its flight. And it was with surprise that, as I took my eyes off the prospect and looked down and in the hedge, I saw that I was in a place where lotus and agrimony and vetch were yellow, and the wild rose continued as ever to hesitate between red and white.

The 'something significant' that he feels from the vision which includes those distant, ruinous-looking hills and these near, coloured flowers, is partly explained in a comparable passage from *The South Country*: here he is in Cornwall, and after saying of the sea 'It is not sun-warmed: it is a monster that has lain unmoved by time . . .', he goes on to describe how, on one occasion at dawn

> . . . it was a bristling sea, not in the least stormy, but bristling, dark and cold through the slow colourless dawn, dark and cold and immense; and at the edge of it the earth knelt, offering up the music of a small flitting bird and the beauty of small flowers, white and gold, to those idols [rocks previously described]. They were terrible enough. But the sea was more terrible; for it was the god of whom those rocks were the poor childish images, and it seemed that the god had just then disclosed his true nature and hence the pitiful loveliness of the flowers, the pitiful sweetness of the bird that sang among the rocks at the margin of the kind earth.

The slight flowers and song, the eternal rocks and sea: it is a fact that the division is felt with more or less intensity by many men. No one could be more aware than Thomas that ultimately the kindness of the earth might be shown to be an illusion of all-too-human thinking. But again it is a fact that we can feel it to be kind; everybody understands Gonzalo when on the sinking ship he cries: 'Now would I give a thousand furlongs of sea for an acre of barren ground—long heath, broom, furze, anything.'

A further effect of Thomas's knowledge of otherness was the way in which the ephemerality of human institutions was felt by him. Later discussion will show that this is not a matter of having fixed ideas but of a living habit of experiencing delicately and significantly. At the moment the theme can be indicated in its simpler aspect by two instances from the earlier writing. In *Oxford* he writes:

> I have ever thought the churchyard with a broken cross at Hinksey, and the willows below and the elms above, if one takes George Herbert there, is a better argument for the Church than Jewel and Chillingworth, if the old yew had not seemed the priest of some old superstition still powerful.

The rather odd construction and syntax of this sentence seems to aid the impression that Thomas is giving with one hand and taking away with the other: we feel tempted to insert 'more' in front of 'powerful'. The main import is not, however, obscured: the power of the old yew prevents full acceptance of the 'argument for the Church', the power of the unconscious growing thing looms over the thing humanly created.

The second example is from *Wales*; and through all the mannered eloquence can be felt a real sense of the contrast between what the mines and chapels stand for, and the presence of the finally conquering power:

> And there is Siloh at ——, standing bravely—at night it often seems perilously—at the end of a road, beyond which rise immense mountains and impassable, and, in my memory, always the night and a little, high, lonely moon, haunted for ever by a pale grey circle, looking like a frail creature which one of the peaks had made to sail for his pleasure across the terrible deeps of the sky. But Siloh stands firm, and ventures once a week to send up a thin music that avails nothing against the wind; although close to it, threatening it, laughing at it, able to overwhelm it, should the laugh become cruel, is a company of elder trees, which, seen at twilight, are sentinels embossed upon the sky—sentinels of the invisible, patient, unconquerable powers: or (if one is lighter-hearted) they seem the empty homes of what

the mines and chapels think they have routed; and at midnight they are not empty, and they love the mountain rain, and at times they summon it and talk with it, while the preacher thunders and the windows of the chapel gleam.

In *Typhoon*, Captain MacWhirr appears to the chief mate Jukes as 'the frail and resisting voice in his ear, the dwarf sound, unconquered in the giant tumult'; a dwarf sound, but unconquered. In Thomas it is the unconscious powers that are unconquerable, and his irony, though light and not unkindly, is unmistakably against Siloh, standing firm and sending up 'a thin music that avails nothing against the wind', and against the preacher thundering while the trees laugh outside or talk with the mountain rain.

Rain. 'At all times I love rain', he writes in *The South Country*,

the early momentous thunderdrops, the perpendicular cataract shining, or at night the little showers, the spongy mists, the tempestuous mountain rain. I like to see it possessing the whole earth at evening, smothering civilization, taking away from me myself everything except the power to walk under the dark trees and to enjoy as humbly as the hissing grass, while some twinkling house-light or song sung by a lonely man gives a foil to the immense dark force. I like to see the rain making the streets, the railway station, a pure desert, whether bright with lamps or not. It foams off the roofs and trees and bubbles into the water-butts. It gives the grey rivers a demonic majesty. It scours the roads, sets the flints moving, and exposes the glossy chalk in the tracks through the woods. It does work that will last as long as the earth. It is about eternal business. In its noise and myriad aspects I feel the mortal beauty of immortal things.

An interesting 'rain' anthology could be compiled from Thomas's writings. We are not so much concerned here with the myriad sounds and appearances that are a source of such keen pleasure to him, but with an aspect which makes us, with some knowledge of the 'rain' in Thomas, pause when we come to reread 'At all times I love rain', pause at 'love'. For we know that it is not 'love' he feels either at the thought or the sound of 'the wild peace of rain falling for ever upon land and upon water'; or if it is love it is at the same time solemnity, awe, abstraction.

There is a lengthy passage in *The Icknield Way* about his lying awake at night listening to the rain. It is an interesting piece of impressionistic writing in which the skilfully managed monotonous flow of its rhythms suggests something of that dark mood that frequently absorbed Thomas. I say 'impressionistic' because his endeavour is more that we should surrender to the mood than attend closely to the thought. And yet the thoughts about the annihilating rain, hyperbolical and repetitive as they tend to become, are present with a certain force throughout and are never entirely nullified by the rhetoric. As he lies awake, the sound of the rain is at first pleasant to him, but before he falls asleep

> it had become a majestic and finally a terrible thing, instead of a sweet sound and symbol. It was accusing and trying me and passing judgment.

He lies for a long time listening, 'under the sentence', and at last hears words which seem to be muttered by a ghostly double beside him:

> The all-night rain puts out summer like a torch. In the heavy, black rain falling straight from invisible dark sky to invisible dark earth the heat of summer is annihilated, the splendour is dead, the summer is gone.

He listens to the rain 'piping in the gutters and roaring softly in the trees of the world'; he thinks of it falling on his grave; and

Once I heard through the rain a bird's questioning watery cry—once only and suddenly. It seemed content, and the solitary note brought up against me the order of nature, all its beauty, exuberance, and everlastingness like an accusation. I am not a part of nature. I am alone.

He feels that he is now only a dead heart and brain, no longer adoring the splendour of summer, which he once did although he was unworthy of such beauty. Even memory fails, and

Everything is drowned and dead. . . . There never was anything but the dark rain. Beauty and strength are as nothing to it. Eyes could not flash in it. . . . It alone is great and strong. It alone knows joy. It chants monotonous praise of the order of nature, which I have disobeyed or slipped out of. I have done evilly and weakly, and I have left undone . . . Black and monotonously sounding is the midnight and the solitude of the rain. In a little while or an age—for it is all one—I shall know the full truth of the words I used to love, I knew not why, in my days of nature, in the days before the rain: 'Blessed are the dead that the rain rains on.'

Out of its context we should probably find fault with this not because its concern with the black rain and the grave is in itself morbid—I do not think it is that—but because the extremity of mood and outlook is largely the outcome of an induced indulgence; he is so eloquent. However, they are sleepy meditations that we are dealing with, and we shall not take the lines too seriously in their context in the whole 'rain' passage. The account of the passage that is given here—the flow of Thomas's writing is, of course, broken in the account and so the quality that I have called 'impressionistic' is in part lost—is to suggest the disharmony between nature and himself that Thomas sometimes deplored his awareness of.

At other times it was, rather strangely, a sense of harmony that he felt to be disquieting; in an abstracted state there was a danger of being merged into the stream of things and so losing his identity. In a *Last Sheaf* essay called 'Insomnia', he wakes in the very early morning, while it is yet dark, and hears a robin starting its song. He knows the sound for such, and yet it is unlike any robin's song he has heard 'in daylight, standing or walking among trees'; and he goes on:

> Outside, in the dark hush, to me lying prostrate, patient, unmoving, the song was absolutely monotonous, absolutely expressionless, a chain of little thin notes linked mechanically in a rhythm identical at each repetition. This was not the voluntary personal utterance of a winged sprite that I used to know, but a note touched on the instrument of night by a player unknown to me, save that it was he who delighted in the moaning fir-trees and in my silence. Nothing intelligible to me was expressed by it; since he, the player, alone knew, I call it expressionless.

The light begins to come, but

> the song in the enclosed hush, and the sound of the trees beyond it, remained the same. . . . I remained awake, silently and as stilly as possible, cringing for sleep. I was an unwilling note on the instrument; yet I do not know that the robin was less unwilling. I strove to escape out of that harmony of bird, wind, and man.

His comments on his response to the robin's song are quite different from those that come from the bird's 'questioning watery cry' in The *Icknield Way* passage: the two situations give rise in fact to 'opposite' explanations of the feeling: disharmony in one, harmony in the other. But fundamentally the responses are the same: a sense of the alien, the other, is the source of each.

NATURE AND THE COUNTRY

I am aware that I have heavily stressed this aspect of Thomas's response to nature, and it may be as well to recall at this point what has earlier been said about the prose that expresses a positive joy in the shapes and colours and significances of what we call familiar things. Our emphasis on his feeling for the 'other' must not diminish our sense of that freshness of daylight vision which makes familiar things new. The sense of the other that helped enormously to give his consciousness the kind of depth and delicacy that are revealed in the poetry did not impair his response to the familiar; rather it sharpened and subtilized. The other might be seen and felt in the familiar, but the beauty was thereby not less but more.

It is not surprising that Thomas does not write with any very sustained power about rural civilization, that there is among his books no *Rural Rides*, no *Hodge and His Masters* or *Amaryllis at the Fair*, no book like Sturt's Bettesworth books or *The Wheelwright's Shop*. He knew much about English history and about English writers; he knew parts of the English countryside with an almost unparalleled intimacy; he is always alluding to English country writers: 'Mr Hardy has really done something to quicken and stouten the sense of past times and generations.' His aim in the second of his anthologies, *This England*, is stated in his note:

Building round a few most English poems like 'When icicles hang by the wall',—excluding professedly patriotic writing because it is generally bad and because indirect praise is sweeter and more profound,— never aiming at what a committee from Great Britain and Ireland might call complete,—I wished to make a book as full of English character as an egg is full of meat. If I have reminded others, as I did myself continually, of some of the echoes called up by the name of England, I am satisfied.

One of the best parts of *In Pursuit of Spring* is where he praises Sturt and 'the unlettered pagan English peasant Bettesworth':

> . . . Now, a statue of Frederick Bettesworth might well be placed at the foot of Castle Street [at Farnham], to astonish and annoy, if a sculptor could be found.

Thomas has all this knowledge, then, all this interest and understanding, and yet in his writings he himself is never a rural sociologist. Out of his abounding references to country people, country activities and stories, there can indeed be formed a valuable 'picture of England'; but these themes are not developed so as to become in themselves the central interest.

There is no need to regret this limitation. Obviously Thomas would not have written the poetry he did write if he had been a different man, and the kind of man he was made him the kind of countryman he was. The man who loves the cuckoo and can yet write (in *The South Country*)

> There is not a broad and perfect day of heat and wind and sunshine that is not haunted by that voice seeming to say the earth is hollow under our feet and the sky hollow over our heads

is perhaps not to be expected to fix a steady attention on human affairs, even though Conrad and to a lesser degree Jefferies, assailed by comparable beliefs or doubts, did so. And there are, after all, other ways of looking at a sheep than the farmer's way, or the sociologist's, or the manufacturer's, or the politician's: Thomas encounters an old, lame sheep, lying in a green lane,

> her eyes pearly green and iridescent with an oblong pupil of blackish-blue. . . . She would not budge even when a dog sniffed at her, but only bowed her head and

threatened vainly to butt. She was huge and heavy and content, though always all alone. As she lay there, her wool glistening with rain, I had often wondered what those eyes were aware of, what part she played in the summer harmonies of night and day, the full night heavens and cloudless noon, and the long moist heat of dewy mornings. (*The South Country*)

It is no good regretting that Thomas's 'vision' of rural life does not carry for us the weight of significances that (say) Lawrence's does in *The Rainbow*.

The comparative narrowness of vision—one must stress the 'comparative'—is due ultimately, I think, to two things that work together in him: his sense of transience, and a complete lack of confidence in the civilization he lived in. His pervasive mood made it impossible for him to contemplate with sustained interest all that we mean when we say 'rural civilization'. He was more interested in what his accidental and momentary encounters with countrymen gave to him, and in thinking about their personal unique lives, than in considering them in their relationship to a rural community. He looks for the life in odd-job workers, in travellers, tinkers, tramps, outcasts. In *The South Country* he describes a reaper at work, making the sheaves and building the stooks, but what mainly interests and fascinates him is that the man has had a many-jobbed and wandering life of toil and pleasure against a background of road and down. He writes in *The Heart of England* about Robert Page, thatcher, gardener, hay-maker, woodcutter, hop-worker, inn-frequenter; he praises his gates, so difficult to make well:

He can even make the beautiful, five-barred gates, with their noble top bars, tapered and shaped like a gunstock and barrel.

Page's thatching is unexcelled and his haystacks 'look like churches when they are new, and so they remain'. Then to this actuality—Page is a countryman of the versatile type so beautifully recorded by Sturt—Thomas adds a long fanciful dream as dreamed by Page, and follows up with imagining him as a 'lesser god in some mythology', and gives an account of the many types of men and women who come to worship at his altars. There is a good deal of characteristic Thomas in the chapter, but he has drifted well away from the countryman.

As with people, so with things. Thomas is as aware as anyone of the significance of plough and harrow, barn and rick, in human life. Writing of Jefferies' *Wild Life in a Southern County*, he says:

> Not only is the book richer in material than its predecessor—so rich that it must have a considerable value as a mere record of a certain time and place in English life—but the treatment is richer, more genial and humane. The waggon's history in the sixth chapter, for example, is a good thing. It has a foundation of special knowledge, but not in the narrow manner of a specialist; and upon this foundation there is the writer's experience of life. Thus it has the merit of some ripe craftsman's talk and the permanence of simple writing.

Thomas values the theme, he values what others say on the theme. But when he comes to write about a waggon himself, it is a broken one (in *Wales*) which he sees as part of the beauty of the September evening, and he thinks of the rides it once gave to children, and he relates the decay not to a changing civilization but to the general idea of change and decay. Or it is, in *The Heart of England*, 'a formless but pregnant shadow' under a broad oak, before dawn; and though its 'ponderous wheels and slender, curving timbers and trailing shafts' are mentioned, it is seen mainly as an emblem of something mysteriously emerging from darkness to light and is related to Dis and Persephone as it

> filled the white road with emotion. . . . I could not reproduce the melody or anything like it, with which the old waggon pervaded the farmyard.

The emblem and the melody tend to make the actual recede, or thin it down. And when he writes of tools, though his appreciation is intense and fine, there is usually something else brought in for consideration with the description, as here where he brings in age and time passing:

> The old man's tools in the kitchen are noble—the heavy wrought-iron, two-toothed hoe, that falls pleasantly upon the hard clay and splits it without effort and without jarring the hand, its ash handle worn thin where his hand has glided at work, a hand that nothing will wear smooth; the glittering, yellow-handled spades and forks; the disused shovel with which he boasts regretfully that he could dig his garden when he lived on deep loam in a richer country than this; and still the useless 'hop-idgit' of six tynes—the Sussex 'shim'—which he retains to remind others, and perhaps himself, that he was a farmer once. (*The Heart of England*)

But while his preoccupations and his temperament prevent him from making rural tradition as such a central theme, he does, of course, refer continually to the antiquity of England as he sees and feels it in the countryside, and never misses an opportunity of introducing details suggestive of it: the peat carts he encounters in Somerset, and the 'two mills pounding away' in that same county. He recalls seeing the ancient 'green man':

> Through the open window of another [room], one Mayday, Jack-in-the-Green bounded in to beg a penny,

97

showing white teeth, white eyes, black face, but the
rest of him covered and rippling with green leaves.
(*The Childhood of Edward Thomas*)

He introduces into the little fantastic stories that make up
Four and Twenty Blackbirds—'They are rather English, I
fancy,' he wrote to Garnett—several actual counties, and
names like Daniel Whidden and Harry Hawke, and nick-
names, and country dialogue, and there are hop-drying,
saddlery, cooking, and many flowers, roads, birds, brooks;
among the kings besieging Troy Town in Dorset are
Barnes and Hardy: he was right in thinking his stories
'rather English'. In *The South Country* he speaks of

> the old English sweetness and robustness of an estate of
> large meadows, sound oak trees not too close together,
> and a noble house within an oak-paled park;

and in the same book he describes a farm which expresses
'the utmost kindliness of earth', and the wayfarer

> only knows that centuries of peace and hard work and
> planning for the undreaded future have made it
> possible.

Ben Jonson's 'To Penshurst', full as it is of 'old English
sweetness and robustness', was a favourite poem of Thomas;
he liked it also for its 'opulence and ease three centuries
old'.

The prose frequently expresses a deep sense of loss at
the passing away of old modes of life. There is an account
in *The South Country* of a man who fought a losing battle
against suburban encroachment that involved the destruction of trees and old houses:

> Those elms had come unconsciously to be part of the
> real religion of men in that neighbourhood, and cer-
> tainly of that old man. Their cool green voices as they
> swayed, their masses motionless against the evening or

the summer storms, created a sense of pomp and awe. They gave mystic invitations that stirred his blood if not his slowly working humble brain, and helped to build and to keep firm that sanctuary of beauty to which we must be able to retire if we are to be more than eaters and drinkers and newspaper readers.

Thomas always felt the force of the particular spiritual truth that he there touches upon, and constantly affirmed its value for life. He often expressed his keen sense of the increasing tendency towards rootlessness: leaving London late one evening, he is oppressed and puzzled when he thinks of all the lives going on behind the lighted windows, and he feels a certain 'modern' unrest there: 'Here were people living in no ancient way.' Elsewhere he speaks of the 'blank or shame-faced crowd of discreetly dressed people who might be anywhere to-morrow'. Thinking in another direction, he regrets that 'the life of cities has destroyed at once the necessity and the power to judge the expanse of earth under our eyes', that a man no longer knows the relation of his own district to the system of hills and rivers to which it belongs, the bones of the land, and the roads:

> If we learn to use a map, it is without fundamental understanding, without the savage's or the soldier's or the traveller's grasp; we must have inherited glimmerings of the old power, but they help us chiefly to an æsthetic appreciation of landscape. (*The Icknield Way*)

One of the 'other selves' that Thomas often uses in his writing—this particular one in *The Country* wears 'the everlasting mourning of clerks'—attributes our languor and aimlessness and fretting to the passing away of something that was a kind of religion of nature:

> There is nothing left for us to rest upon, nothing great, venerable, or mysterious, which can take us out of our-

selves, and give us that more than human tranquillity now to be seen in a few old faces of a disappearing generation. To be a citizen of infinity is no compensation for the loss of that tranquillity.

And he goes on to describe a merry, red-faced old man he once met in the woods, and

... every man (and every poet) who was ever any good had a little apple-faced man or woman like this somewhere not very far back in his pedigree. Where else will he get his endurance, his knowledge of the earth, his feeling for life and for what that old man called God?

Thomas, however, on this occasion points out that the clerk's 'There is nothing to rest upon' is not true: the clerk himself, a nature lover, showed that he had nature and the country to rest on.

On the theme of the degeneration and destruction of country life and values, Thomas comes as near to the forthright expression of strong feeling as he ever does. In that same little book, *The Country*, after stating that the countryman is dying out and that 'when we hear his voice, as in George Bourne's (Sturt's) 'Bettesworth Book', it is more foreign than French', he surprises us with his sudden anger:

He [the countryman] had long been in a decline, and now he sinks before the *Daily Mail* like a savage before pox or whisky.

In *Wales*, at 'an irregular, squalid, hideous, ashen town', he meets a scene of destruction: he had at first been interested in the crowd of men swelling over the pavement in a half-moon shape and had liked the lack of self-consciousness about their figures and clothes,

but when I saw at last what they were watching, I thought that I could have rejoiced to have seen them, looking passionate for once, in flames.

They are watching the demolition of 'Quebec',

> a dignified mid-eighteenth-century house, where for
> five generations a decent, stable professional family had
> lived, loved beauty according to its lights, and been
> graceful in its leisure.

The writing passes into sentimental reminiscence and
elaborate mourning in verbal music, partly concealing
but also perhaps suggesting by its very attempt to conceal,
the anger and the bitter sense of loss.

Two interesting but uneven essays, 'Mothers and Sons'
and 'At a Cottage Door' (both from *Rest and Unrest*), show
a similar anger and bitterness at the change which has
come over the Welsh villages and small towns he is re-
visiting. In the estuary of one of these he had bathed
fifteen years before; he describes it as it was then, and
again as it had been only a little time before that, a rural
community with its farms, church, chapel, cottages, and
three mills, 'one among the oaks of each valley'. Now, the
water is polluted by chemical filth; lines of houses straggle
through pasture and ploughland and waste; the trade of
the cocklers is going to be ruined by the sewage that is to
be poured into the estuary. Thomas gives lurid descriptions of hideous old crones who not long ago were country
women:

> ... few had yet quite realized that they were living not
> at the edge of a field but in the bowels of a town.

There is an ostentatious new public house, and

> opposite stood two others, close together, small and
> homely, no longer rural though they belonged to the
> rural days of the village, but squalid from urban usage.

Cheek by jowl with the dirt and squalor are the new
streets and the plate-glass windows, the purpose and the
efficiency:

Everywhere the ideal implicit was that of a London suburb. . . . All were buying what was very cheap, or very showy, or very new, or very much like something else, or much praised as a really good thing.

The shop-walker is a farmer's son. Commerce and the machine are triumphing: the electric trams are

polished, compact, efficient, without limbs. . . . Men and women might be maimed, deformed, decrepit, pale, starved, rotten, but the wheels, the brakes, the brass-work, the advertisements, and the glass windows must be continually inspected and without spot.

It is impossible not to think of Lawrence when we are reading certain parts of Thomas's accounts of urbaniza-tion, of Lawrence's Wiggeston and Tevershall:

The industrial England blots out the agricultural Eng-land. One meaning blots out another. The new England blots out the old England. And the continuity is not organic, but mechanical. (*Lady Chatterley's Lover*)

But though Thomas is bitterly aware of the degeneration, the tone of his writing is in parts dictated by such a dis-gust—he stresses luridly the physical foulness and squalor —that we may feel that the scene and subject that he is dealing with are not solely the source of his dissatisfaction. And apart from that tone, even his stated attitude is not always certain: he hates the amorphousness and the ugliness, he perceives the ominousness of their spreading onset, and yet he is half afraid that his attitude is the wrong one, that the fault is in himself. In his self-distrust he depicts Willy Morgan, the poet of 'Mothers and Sons', as a poor æsthetic creature, setting him in contrast with his busy, hard-working, and cheerful mother, who lives and doesn't fret. Mrs Owen, too, the tin-plater's wife, still lives within the tradition:

'This frying-pan has fried forty pigs,' she remarked, holding back her head from the hissing rashers.

And it is Mrs Owen who is ironical about the narrator, Mr Phillips (who is, of course, an aspect of Thomas):

> 'How many children is it now?'
> 'Still two,' I said.
> 'Two!' she replied with a smile, and wiped the dough from her fingers in her apron: she spoke in genial irony.
> 'You forget that Mr Phillips is a very wise young man, Sarah,' said Mrs Morgan, chidingly.
> 'He will be wiser,' snapped Mrs Owen, 'when he has had ten children and seen five of them go away, and some of them not come back. As for two, two is toys.'

Thomas makes the busy woman, living amid all the squalor—within her house 'everything shone with use'—a shaft against his contemplative dissatisfied self ('a very wise young man, Sarah'), and so again reveals the uncertainty of attitude which is bound to inhibit a continuous and powerful exploration of the 'changing civilization' theme. But though the theme is not developed very comprehensively, the insight and intelligence that he brings to it show that he is sharply and deeply aware of its importance. *Rest and Unrest* was published in 1910.

'Let the National Gallery go, let the British Museum go, but preserve the Morgans and Abercorran House': the writing in *The Happy-Go-Lucky Morgans* is of a kind and quality that makes it forcefully clear that the people and the life it describes stood for something extremely precious to Thomas. Abercorran House was in Balham, but the Morgans who lived in it were 'more Welsh than Balhamitish'. There was a fine rough garden called the Wilderness, and many animals and birds. Most of the friends of the Morgans were of the 'misfit' type: Aurelius the gypsy-man, 'one of the superfluous'; Mr Torrance the travelling art-master and a 'doomed hack'; Mr Stodham the idealistic clerk. The Morgans themselves and their milieu exemplify some of the qualities and virtues that Thomas prizes:

> In the yard behind, the bull terrier stood for frankness, the greyhound for rusticity, the cats for mystery, and most things for untidiness, and all for ease.

The book is a characteristic Thomas mingling of the actual and the imaginary, of memories and inventive fancies, of descriptions, narrative, legends, dreams, discussions: Thomas called it 'a very loose fiction founded on early memories, of a remarkable Welsh household in London twenty years ago'. Despite some lapses into triviality it is one of the most delightful and best sustained of Thomas's prose books, and its admitted discursiveness need not have made him so apprehensive as he showed himself to be in a letter to Garnett: 'Is the thread too slender, too impudent? Do you even perceive a thread?'

The thread is the Morgan-Abercorran life and the light in which it is seen: the tone of mingled delight and regret that is diffused over the diverse material gives at least an atmospheric unity:

> For the trees are every one of them gone, and with them the jackdaws. The lilies and carp are no longer in the pond, and there is no pond. I can understand people cutting down trees—it is a trade and brings profit—but not draining a pond in such a garden as the Wilderness and taking all its carp home to fry in the same fat as bloaters, all for the sake of building a house that might just as well have been anywhere else or nowhere at all. I think No. 23 Wilderness Street has the honour and misfortune to stand in the pond's place, but they call it LYNDHURST.

There is a certain quiet reflectiveness and clarity in the book that make its tone other than a matter of indulged personal emotion arising out of reminiscence; nevertheless, a sense of personal loss is at the heart of the book. Abercorran House certainly has value for him as a symbol of a merrier, freer, friendlier, less hidebound and less self-righteously respectable life than that typified for him by 'Lyndhurst'; and it does represent an opposition, even though of a passive kind, to the 'world's' encroachments. But, finally, we feel that it is the passing out of his own life of something he has loved that he is fundamentally concerned with, and that the passing of Abercorran House is yet another felt manifestation of the fact of transience that was always coming back to him. It was largely because he tended to envelop what he saw and heard with his sense of transience that he could not bring himself to be interested in civilization in the way that D. H. Lawrence, for instance, was interested; that is, with the profound and searching interest of the artist. Time and again the theme is touched upon in Thomas, and many interesting things are said, and then it is abandoned or modified into something else.

The writings of Thomas and Lawrence ultimately express and embody different life philosophies and metaphysics, but the two men have many things in common. Both have unusual powers of sensuous perception. Both want a fuller and more spontaneous life for man: they do not believe in being 'saved' but in fulfilment. They are in revolt against a rigid adherence to 'ideas', involving as it does the loss of individual life in mass-reactions and routine; they want something better than 'stale thought and coddled emotion' (Thomas). They are enemies of materialism and 'the eternal price list' (Lawrence), at the same time hating poverty and wanting fulfilment for man while he is still on earth. Thomas dislikes, perhaps no less intensely than Lawrence, the 'masters of money-power, with an obscene hatred of life, of true spontaneous life', and would have, like Lawrence, 'a more human system based on life values and not money values' (Lawrence's phrases). These convictions, hopes, dislikes—and there are many more related ones—are stated explicitly in the writings of both men. The fundamental comparison would have to be, of course, between the art that each man achieved, and here Lawrence would be seen to be immeasurably the more powerful. Thomas's sense of the 'gulf' was too pressing to let him achieve a full, firm, complex art like Lawrence's, which in addition to giving a remarkable diagnosis of civilization (a diagnosis that is in part dependent upon his response to nature and his understanding of the response), is in its power and beauty a force to combat the ills and defects he reveals. Nevertheless, the two writers do touch at many points, and sometimes the similarity is quite startling. To look at a number of comparable passages (all of them connected with nature and the country as dealt with in this chapter) will help to get Thomas into perspective as well as furthering our understanding of him, and may be the more interesting if we remember that the two men were almost contemporary, Lawrence being born in 1885, seven years after Thomas. I have not found any reference in Lawrence to Thomas. Thomas reviewed Lawrence's *Love Poems and Others* in *The Bookman* in 1913, and included *Snapdragon* in a selection of poems that he made in 1915 to accompany a publication of coloured drawings entitled *The Flowers I Love* by Katherine Cameron. One would think they might have met during the years (say) 1910 to 1916, which were busy 'literary' years for both of them.

It is not necessary here to demonstrate that the two have much in common in the way of an eye for colour and form in nature, for light and shadow, for atmospheric tones and shades. Many passages could be given that would show similar interests and responses in this particular direction. But it will be profitable to consider a further point of comparison which does not perhaps present itself so readily.

In the following words from *The Heart of England* Thomas refers explicitly to a mode of perception, and to a distinction in perceiving, which we inevitably associate with Lawrence:

> The rain was so dense, and the light so restrained, and the drops hung so about my eyes, and the sound and the sweetness of it made my brain so well contented with all that umber country asleep, that what I saw was little compared with what reached me by touch and by darker channels still.

In his essay 'Art and Morality' (from *Phœnix*), Lawrence might well be explicitly enlarging upon Thomas's 'by touch and by darker channels still':

> When we see a red cow, we see a red cow. We are quite sure of it, because the unimpeachable Kodak sees exactly the same.
>
> But supposing we had all of us been born blind, and had to get our image of a red cow by touching her, and smelling her, hearing her moo, and 'feeling' her? Whatever should we think of her? Whatever sort of image should we have of her, in our dark minds? Something very different, surely!

But though the possibility and the value of the kind of experiencing suggested by these passages are recognized by both Thomas and Lawrence, their final attitudes in the face of it are significantly different. We have seen how Thomas can indicate the strength of his feeling of the *strange* beauty of trees, as in a different and more familiar approach he can tell us clearly and exactly what are the qualities that make the Spanish chestnut tree so good to look at. When it is primarily strangeness that impresses itself upon him—'all the mysterious aloofness of trees', as he says—he tends to be moved to brooding on the strangeness and to stop at that point. Lawrence, on the other hand, is richly nourished and positively activated by his sense of the 'other' in creation; the perception is a source of strength to him. This passage from 'Pan in America' (*Phœnix*) is typical:

> In the days before man got too much separated off from the universe, he *was* Pan, along with all the rest.
>
> As a tree still is. A strong-willed, powerful thing-in-itself, reaching up and reaching down. With a powerful will of its own it thrusts green hands and huge limbs at the light above, and sends huge legs and gripping toes down, down between the earth and rocks, to the earth's middle.

As with trees, so with sea, mountains, sky. That Cornish sea, 'bristling, dark and cold through the slow colourless dawn, dark and cold and immense', was felt primarily by Thomas as a vitally significant contrast with and threat to the loveliness of the flowers and the bird at 'the margin of the kind earth'. This interpretation, an intuitive one and, of course, quite valid, has been formed ultimately, I think, by a strong sense of human vulnerability. Now in Lawrence's *Kangaroo*, Richard Lovat Somers, on the seashore at night, is vulnerable too, 'a bit of human wispiness in thin overcoat and thick boots'; but the tremendous sea—

> Great waves of radium swooping with a down-curve and rushing up the shore. Then calling themselves back again, retreating to the mass. Then rushing with venomous radium-burning speed into the body of the land—

doesn't daunt but strengthens. By feeling the full power of the otherness, and realizing in himself the presence of a 'non-human element—non-human gods, non-human human being'—the man loses the sense of human frailness.

Not that otherness, to Lawrence, is always and inevitably strength-giving. The thankfulness felt by Thomas on escaping from the cold and the immensity of the mountains and coming again towards the world he knows can readily be paralleled in Lawrence. The Captain of *The Captain's Doll* is 'very glad' to have made his expedition to the glacier, which he sincerely pronounces 'marvellous'; but he says he prefers a world 'where cabbages will grow on the soil'. And here is Dollie, the 'Princess' in the story of that name, confronted by mountains:

> In front now was nothing but mountains, ponderous, massive, down-sitting mountains, in a huge and intricate knot, empty of life or soul. Under the bristling black feathers of spruce nearby lay patches of white snow. The lifeless valleys were concaves of rock and spruce, the rounded summits and the hog-backed summits of grey rock crowded one behind the other like some monstrous herd in arrest.
>
> It frightened the Princess, it was *so* inhuman. She had not thought it could be so inhuman, so, as it were, anti-life. And yet now one of her desires was fulfilled. She had seen it, the massive, gruesome, repellent core of the Rockies. She saw it there beneath her eyes, in its gigantic, heavy gruesomeness.

She is frightened, then, as she learns something of 'the dread and repulsiveness of the wild'; with all the wonderful beauty, the repulsiveness is not concealed. And these mountains, in frightening her, are something like those that 'haunted the day' for Edward Thomas. But they do not dominate Lawrence. Mountains and other natural forces may frighten or overshadow characters in his writing, frighten not only by what they suggest in themselves but also because they are usually connected with some terrifyingly real experience. But Lawrence himself, personally, is not dominated by them as we feel Thomas often is; he is not moved by them to brooding or passiveness, he turns easily from them to a clear-sighted scrutiny of human life. His consciousness of the savage-seeming other doesn't burden him; he dominates it. The dark day over the Derbyshire hills which Lawrence describes in *Glad Ghosts*, and the little railway station of stone 'deep in the green, cleft hollow', and seeming in the underworld, would have been keenly felt by Thomas. But where Thomas would probably have confined himself to enlarging upon their effect on himself, Lawrence passes easily and naturally away from the scene to a sharp consideration of the man who is awaiting the arrival of the train.

In *The Happy-Go-Lucky Morgans*, Thomas recalls a certain winter evening of his boyhood, telling how he

> pressed his face on the pane to see the profound of deepening night, and the lake shining dimly like a window through which the things under the earth might be seen if you were out. The abyss of solitude below and around was swallowing the little white moon and might swallow me also; with terror at this feeling I turned away.

Then Aurelius the gypsy-man tells him a story; he sleeps, and dreams. When he wakes:

> I went over to the window and looked out. In a flash I saw the outer vast world of solitude, darkness, waiting

eternally for its prey, and felt behind me the little world within that darkness like a lighthouse. I went back to the others.

This simple 'terror' and the desire to escape from it by 'going back to the others' did not, of course, remain always with Thomas. The poetry in particular shows a much more complex state of mind and feeling than that fear-and-escape situation amounts to. But while not forgetting that it is a boyhood experience that is being described, it would not be unfair to suggest that the account presages a certain passiveness, even something of an attitude of retreat, in the adult man: Thomas was past thirty when he wrote the *Morgans*, and in the passage we are dealing with he is clearly making much of the darkness and solitude, the terror. Without in the least attempting to minimize the force of those realities, one may remember that at the end of *Sons and Lovers*, Paul Morel, after his mother's death, goes into the countryside and stands in the quiet, under the stars, which are also seen reflected in the flood waters below. He is poignantly conscious of his loss, and of the night's immensity:

> But yet there was his body, his chest, that leaned against the stile, his hands on the wooden bar. They seemed something. Where was he?—one tiny upright speck of flesh, less than an ear of wheat lost in the field. He could not bear it. On every side the immense dark silence seemed pressing him, so tiny a spark, into extinction, and yet, almost nothing, he could not be extinct. Night, in which everything was lost, went reaching out, beyond stars and sun. Stars and sun, a few bright grains, went spinning round for terror, and holding each other in embrace, there in a darkness that outpassed them all, and left them tiny and daunted. So much, and himself, infinitesimal, at the core a nothingness, and yet not nothing.

Here, the sense of 'night, in which everything was lost', is at least as strong as in Thomas, but though Paul 'could not bear it', there is also an exultation in being a part however tiny of the great unity, and even at the thought of the night itself 'that outpassed them all'; and Paul, at the very end of the novel, 'would not take that direction, to the darkness'; he walks back 'to the faintly humming, glowing town, quickly'. We know that it is to a further phase in his life that he is progressing. And Lawrence himself went on to write *The Rainbow* and *Women in Love*. To Thomas also, of course, came a new strength, the strength out of which the poetry was born; but the power of the darkness and the solitude is still great there.

It would be possible to discuss usefully the proposition that Lawrence's ultimate outlook is positive and Thomas's negative, that there is for Lawrence a sense of reality at the centre of life, and of unreality for Thomas, and it might be shown how that sense in each determined the essence and scope of his writing. But the best effect of such a discussion would probably be to bring home that 'positive' and 'negative', 'reality' and 'unreality', when used as metaphysical terms, are after all only relative, especially where expression in art is concerned. There is, as we have seen, a sense in which the world is for Thomas an abundantly rich display and offering of life and sensuous beauty; and so far he is 'positive'. But when it is a matter of pondering and concluding and formulating beliefs, then he cannot come to anything like the affirmation that Lawrence gives, for instance, to Birkin in *Women in Love*, as he contemplates the body of his friend Gerald, who has died in the snow. Lawrence there expresses his sense of 'the vast, creative non-human mystery', which could 'bring forth miracles, create utter new races and new species, in its own hour, new forms of consciousness, new forms of body, new units of being'. Thomas never writes of such possible consummations. It is some measure of his quality that we shall listen, when the poetry comes to be considered, with equal seriousness to a voice that has behind it a very different 'belief' from that expressed by Birkin:

> Only an avenue, dark, nameless, without end.

Many excerpts could be assembled from the two writers to show a similarity of attitude towards a world which has become 'too much separated off from the universe'. When Thomas writes, in *The Country*,

> Myths have been destroyed which helped us to maintain a true and vivid acknowledgement of the mystery of the past

we may recall Lawrence's

> For oh I know in the dust where we have buried
> The silenced races and all their abominations
> We have buried so much of the delicate magic of life.
>
> *(Cypresses)*

Also from *The Country*, we have:

> Formerly no one had any idea that the stars were a certain number of million miles away. They entered into human life: they were beautiful and useful, and mythology made them more human but not less godlike. Now they are inferior to gas and electric light.

The author of that would have profoundly understood the author of this:

> . . . somewhere within us the old experience of the Euphrates, Mesopotamia between the rivers, lives still. And in my Mesopotamian self I long for the sun again, and the moon and stars, for the Chaldean sun and the Chaldean stars. I long for them terribly. Because *our*

sun and *our* moon are only thought-forms to us, balls of gas, dead globes of extinct volcanoes, things we *know* but never feel from experience. (*Phoenix*: from a review of Frederick Carter's *The Dragon of the Apocalypse*)

And Lawrence, with his frequent references to the passing of the old cosmic religions which involved an effort to reach direct contact with earth-life, sun-life, cloud-life, rain-life, would have found in Thomas another man who knew that in ancient times men felt that 'the hills and waters were alive with an unknown life' (*The Country*). In *The Last Sheaf* Thomas speaks of himself, rising from drinking at a stream, as 'having caught, and perhaps lost again, a faint sense of the old reverence for springs and running water'.

This glimpse or understanding of the feeling that informed ancient nature religions was for both men a factor making for dissatisfaction with the orthodox Christian conception of God. Lawrence puts it simply enough in his poem 'Fish'; after a description of the fish he has caught, a description emphasizing the strange 'other', he says:

> And my heart accused itself
> Thinking: I am not the measure of creation.
> This is beyond me, this fish.
> His God stands outside my God.

Thomas speaks just as explicitly through the mouth of 'The Friend of the Blackbird', in the essay with that title, from *The Last Sheaf*:

> After reading a book in which a liberal and gentle soul created a liberal and gentle Deity, and showed the necessity for his own adherence to the religion of his fathers, his only comment was: 'It is a good book . . . a good God, but not a very great God after all. . . . What does that thrush say? We must consider him.'

Both Thomas and Lawrence detest (and from a standpoint that has nothing to do with politics) the exploitation of men and nature for merely utilitarian ends. They care unsentimentally about a creature's individual life; the criterion of mere usefulness, the assumptions lying behind the modern overriding emphasis on instrumentality, disgust and appal them. In Thomas the feeling usually finds expression in a more or less quiet and bitter irony, as in the previously quoted passage about the excessive care shown for the electric trams, and in the passage about the sheep which 'only in their lambhood and motherhood are obviously of a different tribe from sausage-machines'. It may seem a far cry from Thomas's dry statement to the force of the magnificent invective in 'Aristocracy', where Lawrence is attacking the all-too-human interpretation of the great natural realities; but the motive for protest is fundamentally the same:

> . . . Was not the ram created before you were, you twaddler? Did he not come in might out of chaos? And is he not still clothed in might? To you, he is mutton. Your wonderful perspicacity relates you to him just that far. But any farther, he is—well, wool.
>
> Don't you see, idiot and fool, that you have lost the ram out of your life entirely, and it is one great connection gone, one great life-flow broken? Don't you see you are so much the emptier, mutton-stuffed and wool-wadded, but lifeless, lifeless?

Thomas does not write with such a force of anger and humour, but the old sheep in the grassy lane, with 'eyes pearly green and iridescent with an oblong pupil of blackish-blue', and which he wondered over—'what part she played in the summer harmonies of night and day, the full night heavens and cloudless noon, and the long moist heat of dewy mornings'—is not so very far removed from Amon, the great ram.

A good deal has already been said of the evidence, as perceived by Thomas, of disintegration in the rural community and of his attitude towards it. It is true that he was not always sure whether he was right in unreservedly hating the industrial amorphousness, and that there were moments when he thought his hatred of ugliness might be due to what he feared he had in him of the 'aesthete'. And sometimes he wondered with his David Morgan whether the city thousands, 'lacking as their life might be in familiar forms of beauty and power', did not possess 'a profound unconsciousness and dark strength which might some day bring forth beauty'. But mostly he saw them as 'held in a vice of reserve or pallidly leering. . . . They had not been given a chance. . . . They had no gods, only a brand-new Gothic church' (*The South Country*). And in the details, the significant details, that they give of the 'new' environment, the two authors are sometimes curiously alike, even to verbal correspondences. The description (from *Lady Chatterley's Lover*) of the car journey through 'the long squalid straggle of Tevershall', gives us

> mud black with coal-dust, the pavements wet and black. . . . The stacks of soap in the grocers' shops, the rhubarb and lemons in the green-grocers! the awful hats in the milliners! all went by ugly, ugly, ugly,. followed by the plaster and gilt horror of the cinema with its wet picture announcements, 'A Woman's Love', and the new big Primitive chapel, primitive enough in its stark brick and big panes of greenish and raspberry glass in the windows. . . .

In Thomas's accounts of the scene and spiritual climate of the old-new Welsh villages and towns we get things like this, from *Rest and Unrest*: '. . . straggling lines of houses running far out and up into the pasture and ploughland

and waste'; and from *Wales*: '. . . the black, wet roads; the ugly houses . . . the cheap and pretentious chapels'. And he writes in *The Icknield Way*:

> In these new towns I see women looking as if they were made in the chemists' shops, which are so numerous and conspicuous in the streets.

In contrast to this environment and trend and to the humanity that are produced by it—though neither Thomas nor Lawrence offers naïve panaceas for the state of things they see as bad—there are country people whose lives have firmer foundations. Of a farmer (in *The South Country*), 'a thick bent, knotty man, with bushy dark hair and beard and bright black eyes', Thomas writes:

> Life is a dark simple matter for him; three-quarters of his living is done for him by the dead; merely to look at him is to see a man five generations thick, so to speak, and neither Nature nor the trumpery modern man can easily disturb a human character of that density. . . . He has the trees as well as his ancestors at his back.

Life is probably not quite such a 'dark simple matter' for this man as Thomas suggests; but the 'density' and the unconscious inherited wisdom are certainly facts and are serviceable for living. In the opening pages of *The Rainbow*, Lawrence's presentment of the interrelation of the Brangwens with the 'heaven and earth' that 'was teeming around them', similarly stresses a 'thickness' and strength in the life and consciousness of the country people:

> . . . and the limbs and the body of the men were impregnated with the day, cattle and earth and vegetation and sky, the men sat by the fire and their brains were inert, as their blood flowed heavy with the accumulation from the living day.

Neither writer, of course, postulates this dark strength as the be-all and end-all of human life: Thomas is as interested in the fine consciousness as in the 'thick bent, knotty man', and Lawrence in that same book—to say nothing of his subsequent writings—goes on to present a development and branching out of the Brangwen life through three generations. Both writers know that to live by tradition alone would be stagnancy. But both know also that rural living could produce a firmness and whole-someness which are at the other extreme to the nervous condition of Thomas's schoolmaster (in *Wales*):

> The ghosts of the subtle emotions which we say make up modernity have come into his brain, and they are so many that he has become, if not a theatre, at least a mortuary, of modernity. But the nervous strain of any real passion in his neighbourhood obliges him to be rude or to run away.

What may have seemed a large claim was made for Thomas's nature prose in the first paragraph of this chapter: it was there suggested that 'in certain aspects there is not a nature writer in the language who surpasses him'. I had in mind the quality of the vision whose beauty comes from the union of a sensuous perceptiveness unusual in its delicacy and variety (the born gift cultivated by an intensity of interest and love), with the peculiar response to the 'other' in nature, the whole being infused or coloured with certain habits of thought which make its individuality both more distinct and more subtle.

H. J. Massingham, writing of *The Icknield Way* in *Through the Wilderness*, seems surprised to have to make the comment that 'its archæological knowledge and interest are of the vaguest'. But the subjectiveness that he—himself a country writer of much knowledge (and often also of an admirable and valuable ardour)—is by unconscious implication regretting, is also Thomas's strength. The ancient tracks over the Downs, no less than the trees and flowers and creatures, and no less than the sky and the shape and motion of clouds, and the remoteness of twilight at evening and dawn, were apprehended by him in a mode which far transcended 'knowledge and interest' as the words are ordinarily used. And clearly if his approach had been more abstract and factual, we should have lost something of the feeling of a personality that his nature writing gives. Edward Thomas's experience of nature was intensely personal.

CHAPTER FOUR

Literary Criticism

IN bulk, Edward Thomas's literary criticism surpasses both his nature writings and his collections of general essays. There are the full-length critical studies of Jefferies, Pater, Swinburne, Maeterlinck, Borrow, and the lengthy *Feminine Influence on the Poets*, and the smaller books on Keats and Lafcadio Hearn; there are numerous reviews and articles and 'Introductions', and there is the incidental criticism that occurs in the nature books and elsewhere. Much of this critical work was commissioned, and the necessity of producing a prearranged number of words was undoubtedly at times the main cause of faults like repetitiveness and the inclusion of insignificant bio-graphical detail. But Thomas was a conscientious writer, and whether the work was commissioned or not he never spared himself thought and the effort to give of his best. And that he had a fine critical mind is as clear as the fact that conditions made it difficult for that mind to produce always of its best.

As a reviewer in need of money, Thomas was obliged to do a lot of reading; but he had already from early days read widely and from choice in English literature. More-over, it is clear that he naturally and lightly exer-cised a critical habit of mind in the circumstances of his daily life: his writings are full of his observation of people and of comments and speculation about their lives, to say nothing of remarks on pictures, furniture, public monuments, epitaphs, architecture and so on.

The small book on Keats, containing a good deal of matter—family history, etc.—that is of little critical relevance, was written for a series called 'The People's Books'. The *Jefferies*, on the other hand, is a full and thorough critical study. Similarly, the *Pater* is a more important book than that on the unusual but very minor Lafcadio Hearn. The *Feminine Influence on the Poets* contains much good criticism of poetry as well as interesting general comment, whether he is dealing with Shakespeare or Donne or Wordsworth or the array of women poets whose names are not likely to be known to us. But it is a patchy book, and the chapter headings suggest the kind of build-up that it is: The Inspiration of Poetry; Women and Inspiration; Women as Poets; Women, Nature, and Poetry; Passion and Poetry; Mothers of Poets; Poets and Friendly Women; The Tenth Muse; Patronesses. Nevertheless, in spite of this odd assortment and of many pages of unimportant biographical fact, The *Feminine Influence* has enough of freshness to make it well worth attention. The other full-length books too, particularly the *Swinburne*, have some fine insights and critical demonstrations. It is chiefly in his shorter pieces and incidental references that there is sometimes a serious slackening of critical attention.

There is no lack of variety in approach. Passages abound that show his profound regard for beauty and sincerity in life and in writing: his own values for life and living are here forcefully apparent. There is discussion of themes such as the individual use of words (as opposed to the stale and general); the value a word may have by virtue of ancient and racial usage; how words may lose power with time; the corruption of language; the essential effect of rhythm; stock responses (not worded in that way, of course); the writer's relation to tradition; impersonality in writing, and so on. There is the frequent use of that part of intelligence which we loosely call psychological insight:

> Jefferies' illness, by confining his physical activity and putting a keener and more perilous edge upon his sensitiveness, threw him back still more upon himself.

He can amuse himself in a review of Wilcox (Ella Wheeler) —'one says "Wilcox" just as one says "Shakespeare" '— whom we cannot ignore because she speaks for 'large bodies of her fellow-creatures':

> It is impossible to tell if she prefers amorous excesses or 'scattering seeds of kindness', or would combine both. Her breadth is great. . . . Wilcox is not ashamed to repeat. . . . Like Shakespeare, she is a plagiarist, but her motive—to do good and to sell—justifies her, as art would not.

(Her vogue was, of course, enormous; the review belongs to 1913.) He can be terse about Borrow: 'He spoke thirty languages and translated their poetry into verse.' He is fond of quoting illuminating stories or incidents, like that one of Cobbett, who, it will be remembered, when threatened with expulsion from a meeting, 'rose, that they might see the man they had to put out'. Sometimes he is discursive, sometimes close and exacting. His approach is sometimes unduly historical or biographical; on the other hand, he can direct a most acute analytical faculty to sentences and single words.

Though for one reason or another there are hesitations and mixed judgments in some places of Thomas's criticism, in fundamentals his likes and dislikes are to be clearly seen.

He consistently deplores a predominantly spectatorial attitude towards life. Of Pater he writes:

> In his mind, as, according to his opinion, in *The Renaissance* generally, there are 'no exclusions'; 'whatsoever things are comely', all are reconciled 'for the elevation and adorning' of his spirit; he recognizes no essential incompatibility between any really beautiful things, between the freshness of a youthful art and the 'subtle and delicate sweetness' of a 'refined and comely decadence'. He hardly distinguishes between life and art: as they reach his mirror they are alike. . . . He is a spectator. His aim is to see: if he is to become something it is by seeing.

And this 'aesthetic' kind of seeing is then shown to involve a lack of real sympathy, a lack which Thomas feels to be deplorable and even deadly but which he nevertheless handles often with a light touch. He dislikes 'these noble attitudes, these tragical situations which thrilled the Fellow of Brasenose. One more step, and he would bid the dying gladiator be comforted by the stanzas of Childe Harold.' Clearly and ironically exposing the central flaw in Pater's whole attitude, he suggests the kind of harshness and rigidity which results from the ultra-aesthetic approach to life. Pater 'tends to turn all things great and small into a coldly pathetic strain of music'.

The same alienation from life is seen in much of the writing of Maeterlinck and Lafcadio Hearn, and it is coldness that is emphasized in the 'dainty unreality' of the 'trivial vicar', Herrick. For Thomas, Herrick's 'miniature delicacy' counts for little in the absence of human warmth: 'Literature, Greek, Latin, and English, would have given him nine-tenths of what he says of women', of whom he writes 'as if they were no more animate than their scented clothes'.

The aloofness from real life that Thomas is concerned to make us see as disabling for writers, is shown to go frequently with an undue subjectiveness and a tendency to

'refinement'. One of his key criticisms of Swinburne is that
that poet is unable or unwilling to give the object its due,
to contemplate and present without covering it over with
his own traits or desires or feelings. Of the famous description of the bees' flight in *La Vie des Abeilles*, he says: 'It
brings before me not so much the bee as the poet admiring
the bee.' And he indicates (also in *Maeterlinck*) the
emotional thinness that may come of excessive preoccupation with one's feelings: 'The pallor and melancholy are
parts of the writer's refinement. . . . If there is anything
here to be called sorrow it is no more passionate than
wall-paper.'

Thomas is as careful to note unbalance in temperament
and emotion as he is to point to inadequacy of experience
or falsification of fact. And when he writes about these
departures from a norm of sanity and 'reality' he never
fails to provide ample supporting detail. He picks out as
the worst fault of *Endymion* 'the expressions of incontinent,
soft feeling, the languors and luxuries': it is as if Keats
himself, like Endymion, had 'swooned Drunken from
pleasure's nipple'. Pater's refined-emotive use of language
(on occasions) is distasteful as revealing disproportionate
or inappropriate feeling:

> . . . Thus he [Pater] speaks of a 'ghastly shred' picked
> from dead bones by somebody who did not think it
> 'ghastly'; and this is made the more intrusive by the
> presence of the word 'ghastly' half a page back, and
> 'shocking' immediately after.

'These are flaws of style', adds Thomas, at the same time
showing abundantly that they are flaws of sensibility also.
He suggests Shelley's limiting subjectivity when he says of
him: 'His ideas were stronger than his surroundings.'

Actuality, tangibility, truth to one's 'surroundings', are
not overriding considerations with Thomas, but he always

points to a departure from them when such a departure seems to him to have regrettable consequences. Meredith's 'The Lark Ascending' is praised for the real bird with which it begins, but finally 'he gets at least as far away from the bird as Shelley does, if he starts closer'; and in general Meredith 'got away from the Earth and things of the Earth to intellectual analogues of them'. In Hazlitt's nature writing, too, we have, says Thomas, 'a glorious idea of the earth rather than the earth itself'. And he has no difficulty in demonstrating the error of a critic who praised Blake's *Milton* for being 'redolent of the countryside . . . the plough and harrow'; he shows that the plough in that instance never lay outside Blake's door at Felpham.

He is careful to expound clearly whatever kind of inadequacy of experience he may have detected in the writing before him. The early stories of Jefferies have 'much facility and exuberance of trashiness', for Jefferies is not yet equipped emotionally or intellectually for the subjects he has chosen: 'His subjects lay outside of him, quite apart; or they had entered into his heart, not his mind.' Pater's assumption of experience—'the animalism of Greece', etc.—is seen to be somewhat grotesque when we take account of what he actually understood and of what his actual life was: 'Pater lived a sober, almost ascetic life at Oxford, varied by tours in continental churches and galleries with his sisters.' Thomas, whose own writing was for so long influenced by Pater, came finally to recognize his shortcomings in full, while characteristically paying tribute wherever he could. He concentrates not on Pater's life but on his writings, and in addition to the value that his central criticisms have, his analyses of Pater's 'style', of his diction and images and rhythms, are acute and rewarding.

Inflated feeling, exaggerated gestures, condescension,

posturing, grossness, bad temper are seen by Thomas as faults in writing that spring from, ultimately, flaws in character. As early as 1902 he writes in a letter that Rossetti

> expresses his emotion if at all by the sound of the words and not by their meaning. His sonnets are often like big men in pompous clothing. They are impressive without saying anything.

Of Swinburne's sonnets on 'the worm Napoleon', he says, 'the hissing, spitting, and cursing is the frantic abuse of a partisan'. Keats's poems to Fanny Brawne are 'frantic personal pieces', and much of *Endymion* is marked by 'a too easy voluptuousness'. On the other hand, Swift, who 'was not a poet, nor was he a very skilful or brilliant versifier', erred in a direction still more regrettable, for usually

> the thought of women only impels him to exceed in the cold, the callous, and the gross in that combination which is Swift's alone.

Though extremely generous, Thomas is not a hero-worshipper in criticism: where occasion warrants he is quietly and unaggressively firm. Of Jefferies (of whom he is as fond as he is of Keats) he can say: 'He made a hundred mistakes, narrow, ill-considered, splenetic, fatuous'. Borrow (another favourite though with serious reservations) 'saw himself as a public figure that had to be treated heroically', and in *Wild Wales* he is 'nearly always the big clever gentleman catechizing certain quaint little rustic foreigners'. The recurrence of Borrow's Man in Black (in *Lavengro*) is an instance of the obsessiveness which Thomas never fails to point out as a deviation from good sense and proportion. He notes in Hardy (whose poems he preferred to the novels)

. . . that most tyrannous obsession of the blindness of
Fate, the carelessness of Nature, and the insignificance
of Man, crawling in multitudes like caterpillars, twitched
by the Immanent Will hither and thither.

He finds a 'perversity' in Hardy's over-use of irony.

Vaguenesses and confusions of meaning come in for
sharp analysis. In Swinburne, for instance, there are the
'inexcusably amplified similes', some of them carried so
far that 'the matter of the simile is more important in the
total than what it appeared to intensify'. 'Exact correspondence is wanting' in many of them. Thomas is particularly severe on what he calls the 'confusion of categories and indefinite definiteness of images', the indis-
criminate mingling of incongruous elements, as in 'sand
and ruin and gold', and 'hours of fruitful breath'; he
shows that in a phrase like 'snows and souls', 'snows'
lowers the value of 'souls'. Swinburne

> will say that a woman is 'clothed like summer with
> sweet hours', but that at the same time her eyelids are
> shaken and blue and filled with sorrow.

He comments on the comparative emptiness of a phrase
like 'bright fine lips', pointing out that the adjectives are
'complimentary and not descriptive':

> Swinburne admired brightness, and he called a woman's
> lips 'bright' and in the next stanza but one a blackbird
> 'bright'. I do not know what 'fine' means, but I suspect
> that it is not more definite than the vulgar 'fine' and
> his own 'splendid'.

But despite his exactingness and his finding so much in
Swinburne that 'is almost maddening to the soberly in-
quiring intelligence', he contrives to say a good deal on
the credit side and it is not likely that we shall consider
his all-over estimate of that poet to be ungenerous.

Some excellent remarks on Pater's prose show how Thomas relates the lack of flow, of inevitable development, in the writing, to the author's character and tendencies, in the same way that he sees Swinburne's peculiar energies finding expression in his varied metres and stanza forms. He sees the

> stiffness, the lack of an emotional rhythm in separate phrases, and of progress in the whole, the repellent preoccupation with an impersonal and abstract kind of perfection,

as the inevitable effect of Pater's 'shy and rigid spirit'; and 'when his prose sounds well it is with a pure sonority of words that is seldom related to the sense'. The lack of a meaningful continuous flow is associated at the same time with Pater's 'spectatorial attitude' and his incessant striving for 'visible' effects in the manner indicated here:

> When he has to say that Leonardo was illegitimate, he uses eight words: 'The dishonour of illegitimacy hangs over his birth.' He at once makes the 'dishonour' a distinction with some grandeur: he almost makes it a visible ornament.

Pater is by no means dismissed: 'Open any essay at any page: it will yield some beautiful object or strange thought presented in the words of a learned and ceremonious lover.' But in the end Pater's works are 'a polished cabinet of collections from history, nature, and art'; and we are not surprised that the writing which comes of such limited and chilly experience should be marked by 'the lack of progressive movement, the lack of a clear and strong emotional tone such as makes for movement'.

First-hand experience and its accompanying freshness and reality of feeling; full knowledge of one's material, and precision with flow in the expression of it; the energies and vitality and interests which make for our sharper taste and ultimately our deeper delight in life: such (in the broadest terms) are what he wants in litera- ture and what he has the necessary understanding and knowledge to indicate and demonstrate in a wide variety of writers. (It is interesting that his criticism was con- sidered by his contemporaries to be too searching: R. P. Eckert says, 'Thomas's kindliest critics wrote that he showed a taste too fastidious and a judgment too severe'.)

To Thomas, the immense superiority of Shakespeare's sonnets over those of his contemporaries lies in the strength of passion that they express, and it seems certain to him that the passion is directly 'autobiographical':

> Shakespeare's sonnets, from 'In the old age black was not counted fair' onwards, appear to be most of them far more than usual directly related to facts of present or very recent experience.

But while so strongly attracted by that strength, and so much concerned to show it to others as an admirable and a great thing, he is still the discriminating critic:

> 'In the old age' itself is not one of these (i.e. the greater sonnets), and there are others such as 'My mistress's eyes are nothing like the sun', where some of the lines are too much like the hundred thousand other Eliza- bethan sonnets to have an individual effect.

He does indeed assign tremendous value to the best of the sonnets, to the power and truth of their revelations:

> The lack of anything that might even seem to be decoration gives the series to the Dark Lady an extreme power, exchanging for Shakespeare's customary sensu- ousness of language the undraped sensuousness and still greater sensuality of the man himself. . . . They do not, or hardly at all, make any appeal to the indolent love of poetry.

And he goes on to suggest that other Elizabethan sonneteers perhaps had not Shakespeare's 'abandonment or lack of shame; at any rate their expression followed their experience afar off'. They may have had strong feelings, but they were 'poor writers, men with an impassable door between their poetry and their individual life, men who could not be sincere with the best will in the world except when compelled in a state of excitement to utter plain prose'.

Donne also is praised for poetry which is marked by the note of deep individual experience:

> It was Donne's distinction to be the first after Shakespeare, and almost at the same time as Shakespeare, to write love poems in English which bear the undeniable signs not only of love but of one moment of love and for one particular woman. His poems to his wife are of the same kind. There is none of the old-fashioned generalization in them at all.

Landor's 'marmoreal nothings' about love (Landor 'who knows nothing between the lofty exalted womanliness which he might have borrowed from literature and the kittenish vacuity which looks as if it might be what he was used to in living women') are contrasted with the songs of Burns, where the women have 'an outdoor grace' and 'will stand the sunlight and the breath of life'. Burns, too, has his Chloris and his Clarinda, but the lightness and freshness of his best love poetry are the expression of a spontaneity of spirit which is beautiful:

> Spirit and body are one in it—so sweet and free is the body and so well satisfied is the spirit to inhabit it.

These poems

> seem always to be the fruit of a definite and particular occasion. They are not solitary poetry like 'I can give

not what men call love', which never was to be spoken
except to the unpeopled air.

Byron is not so far from Landor as Burns is, 'but still far
enough away': Landor and Byron are 'alike chiefly in
their worldly position and the way they took advantage
of it; but Byron, though he could stoop to Claire Clair-
mont and then treat her, the mother of his child, with
studied frigidity for years, could yet abandon himself to
his passion with a frankness which has its admirable side;
nothing of the kind is recorded of Landor'. He concludes
his remarks on Byron—they are in *Feminine Influence on the
Poets*, as are the comments on the other poets referred to
in this paragraph—by saying that it was part of his 'great
power'

> to keep his verse always in touch with the actual world
> of his own time, to allow the circulation of blood be-
> tween his poetry and his world of flesh, shone upon by
> the very sun and blown across by the living winds.

This insistence on the great value of 'reality' is not, of
course, equivalent to a (naïve) demand for realism. Certainly he is inclined on occasions to discuss overmuch the
connection of writing with the outward circumstances of
the writer's life, but he never depends for his judgment
upon detecting that connection; a connection that is
visibly close is not necessarily a guarantee of 'truth' for
him. The truth that matters most has to be found in the
writing itself.

The attention Thomas gives to 'reality' comes of his
dislike of the manufactured and the 'aerial' (his word) in
attitudes and emotion. In this connection there is an
interesting passage in *Feminine Influence* that touches upon
the question of the writer's relation to tradition. After
regretting that in England 'during the Renaissance the
natural was almost obscured by the pastoral in the formal

poetry of love', he shows how in Scotland a stout pro-
vincialism survived in the songs, helping to preserve a
lively and firm reality: 'Their women are Scotch women',
he writes, 'and their country is Scotch country, but it
cannot be said of the women or the country in many English poets between the Renaissance and the Romantic
Revival that they are English.' There is, obviously, more
to be said than that, and Thomas himself is perfectly
aware of the possibility of expressing 'sincerity' without
being naturalistic; but on balance his insistence on the
kind of reality in question seems wholly salutary.

Even in the early (1817) volume of Keats it is the poet's
'exceptional fidelity to his own thought, feeling, and
observation' that he emphasizes most:

> Very few pieces are exercises in sentiment. In the great
> majority he is curiously and deliberately true to the
> facts of outward form and inward feeling.

Similarly, Keats' letters are 'excelled by none in their
direct presentation of the moment's phases of mind and
moods of temperament'. But it is in the *Jefferies* that these
particular qualities receive most attention. This doesn't
mean that Jefferies is for Thomas the greatest of writers;
Thomas points continually to limitations and defects in
him. But Jefferies does abundantly display those virtues of
'truth' and 'sincerity'. Of *The Gamekeeper at Home* Thomas
writes: 'He knows it all perfectly well, and talks about it
with a rich, quiet ease'; *Hodge and His Masters*, flawed as
it is, says the critic, by partisanship, nevertheless 'tells in
the end by its weight of wide and intimate knowledge'; all
through *Wild Life in a Southern County*, Jefferies 'sees things
as they are, without a tinge of pastoral or other sentiment'.
The kestrel's hovering, says Thomas, is described by
Jefferies with an exactness and a vividness till then un-

known in that kind of writing (it is characteristic of his own carefulness and sobriety that he adds, 'True it is that it is bound to be superseded by something yet more exact and as vivid'); and on Jefferies' stating that you do not see the purple in ripe wheat if you look specially for it, but that 'when the distant beams of sunlight travelling over the hill swept through the ripe rich grain, for a moment there was a sense of purple on the retina', Thomas's comment is: 'The honesty and exactness of that guarantee the quality of his work and of his observation.'

It is in the intensity of the perceptions, the 'joy' in perceiving even when the mood is sorrowful, that Thomas sees the chief spiritual force of Jefferies, a force conveyed again and again with a 'blissful ease and sincerity'. He emphasizes the 'deeply piercing' quality of *The Story of My Heart*; the overflowing generosity of feeling in the book does not blind Thomas to the faults in it, but that feeling counts overwhelmingly in his sense and estimate of the whole. He demonstrates that in essays like 'Meadow Thoughts' and 'The Pageant of Summer',

> Nature's loveliness, permanence and abundance is married to the writer's humanity in a manner that effects a more rare and more difficult achievement—one of Jefferies' greatest achievements—than the pictures of Ruskin or of Stevenson.

Some of Thomas's best criticism occurs when he is showing how his author enhances our sense of life; and the fineness of this criticism comes of his own seriousness: ultimately it is from the seriousness that the insight springs. Of course, sensuous beauty is everywhere celebrated, whether it is in the simple earliest Keats, which is

> full of his delight, fresh from the meadows, brooks, and copses, in pretty things, in blossoms, birds, fishes

(where 'pretty', while suggesting Thomas's estimate of the poetry, does not necessarily modify the delight), or in *The Eve of St Agnes*, of which he says,

> In fact it is impossible to suppose that poetry of this immobile, sumptuous, antiquarian kind can go beyond it

or in a passage like

> The Naiad 'mid her reeds
> Press'd her cold finger closer to her lips

which is 'visible and alive'. Jefferies has as much as Keats of this particular delight, but it is seen also as only a part of a larger response to and a larger grasp of life:

> ... But five senses are not the sum even of a sensual man, and in Jefferies they are humble in the service of the soul that apprehends the beauty of life and the bitterness because that must fade or die by the hand of Fate or Time or Man himself.

It is the 'soul's' living reverence for life which Thomas finds expressed with such force and abundance in Jefferies; and one says 'living' so that no hint of solemn religiosity may creep in and attach itself to the phrase.

Again and again Jefferies is shown as speaking for life. The chapter headed 'Last Essays' has much to say about the 'narrow sectarians' who endeavoured to make capital out of Jefferies' alleged last words as he was dying, and after some forceful and ironical remarks it ends with saying:

> The majority will be those who, orthodox Christians or not, see in the work of Jefferies, when he was most alive, a force at one with the good that is in the world, with what makes for wisdom, beauty, and joy, whether it can usefully be connected with Christianity or not.

In *Amaryllis*, 'Jefferies has free play for all his nature'; he is praised for his quick, wide, and flexible understanding:

> Restless and sad and gay and wonderfully kind was the humanity that saw the Idens and the Flammas thus; that painted them stroke by stroke, correcting or enhancing earlier effects, until the whole thing breathed.

And his recognition of a further trait in Jefferies that makes for life—his insistence on the importance of the present and the future—and the way of dealing with that recognition are themselves suggestive of the quality of Thomas's own seriousness:

> His asserted lack of tradition, his rebuke of the past, his saying that the old books must be rewritten, is a challenge to the present to take heed of itself. There is no real lack of a sense of the past in one who has a sense of co-operation with the future, which adds to the dignity of life, gives a social and eternal value to our most solitary and spiritual acts, and promises us an immortality more responsible than that of the theologians, as real if not as flattering.

Best of all, perhaps, in this direction and approach is a passage that comes near the end of the book:

> His lonely, retiring, and yet emphatic egoism made a hundred mistakes, narrow, ill-considered, splenetic, fatuous. He was big enough to take these risks, and he made his impression by his sympathies, his creation, not by his antipathies. He drew Nature and human life as he saw it, and he saw it with an unusual eye for detail and with unusual wealth of personality behind. And in all of his best writing he turns from theme to theme, and his seriousness, his utter frankness, the obvious importance of the matter to himself, give us confidence in following him; and though the abundance of what he saw will continue to attract many, it is for his way of

seeing, for his composition, his glowing colours, his ideas, for the passionate music wrought out of his life, that we must chiefly go to him. He is on the side of health, of beauty, of strength, of truth, of improvement in life to be wrought by increasing honesty, subtlety, tenderness, courage, and foresight. His own character, and the characters of his men and women, fortify us in our intention to live.

How remarkable that Mr Moore can say of Jefferies and of Thomas's book, 'He was an awkward subject for any biographer, and Edward's dull, solid, competent book was as much as, or more than, he deserved'! The more remarkable, perhaps, because Mr Moore was himself a 'country writer'. Though it may be that by the time we come to that statement in his *Life and Letters of Edward Thomas*, we have been warned, by both the tone and substance of many of his remarks, not to be surprised by anything: 'Jefferies was not a very good writer, though he was sometimes a good journalist'; the young Edward Thomas was 'a good little Liberal'; when he courted Helen it was 'in his shy, absurd, and tentative way'; 'in social relationships, in the ways of the world . . . he was a child' with 'hardly a practical thought' in his head, says Mr Moore, writing of the Oxford period. I think those who have a sufficient knowledge of Thomas would agree that to fail to see his early life, including his marriage and the responsibility of children, as more than usually rapid in growth, is as imperceptient and betraying as to use a phrase like 'a year's trivial happenings in field and hedgerow', which Mr Moore applies to Thomas's first nature book. It is not Edward Thomas who is being shown to us in epithets like 'good little', 'absurd', 'a child', and that fantastic 'trivial'.

An opposite judgment on Thomas's *Jefferies* is to be

found in an article by Q. D. Leavis, in *Scrutiny* (March 1938). In the course of reviewing some books of selections from Jefferies, and asking for a Wiltshire Edition of his Collected Works, she has this to say of Thomas's *Life*, which she would like to see introducing the proposed collection:

> This book should be recognized as a classic in critical biography, to stand with Lockhart's Scott and Mrs Gaskell's Brontë in point of intrinsic interest and containing better literary criticism than many critical works. . . . Since subsequent writers on Jefferies take all their facts from him as well as his careful bibliography, generally without acknowledgment, and since there is nothing more to be found out about Jefferies . . . to reprint Thomas's work would automatically render further book-making unnecessary. His is a model biography. The author is recognized as being present only by the sympathy that informs the narrative and the intelligence that directs the criticism and determines the selections. The selections from Jefferies' works there are so abundant and well-chosen that Thomas's Life of itself will send the reader to their sources.

That tribute comes from a disinterested and clear-sighted critic. It is true that Thomas, on finishing the book, wrote to Hudson that he was 'thoroughly sick of it, and it seems wholly bad and full of sound and fury and my special brand of vagueness'. But we know more now than even Hudson did about the (frequent) extremity of Thomas's self-doubt; and we have the book before us. It would be hard to find a better exposition than Thomas's of the life that is in essence rich in being the very antithesis of the merely 'spectatorial'.

Men who, in a more obvious sense than Jefferies, participate in life with 'a personal vigour and courage' come in for a special word from Thomas. Chaucer, Sidney,

Jonson, Drayton, Byron, Morris are named: not all of them among the great, he says, but how we should miss their poems. When he speaks of the 'plain humanity' of Chaucer and Jonson and Byron, it is the sense that they give of a certain robust familiarity with the affairs of life that commends itself to him. He stresses Cobbett's strength of mind, his courage, independence, and straightforwardness: 'Simplicity kept him sweet through the muck of journalism and politics'; and shows that though he spoke with respect of beer, he was no beef-and-beer man:

> His morals were not beef-and-beer morals. It might be shown too that his style, with all its open-air virility, is yet lean and undecorated, in accordance with his shrewd puritanism.

In Dampier's *Voyages*, what impresses him most are the sharp truthfulness—'he had an eye for everything'—and the sympathy: 'His knowledge of the Indians and other strange people, and his sympathy with them, are rare and beautiful to see'; and Thomas has 'a very pleasant sense of the man himself', in this 'fine, vivid, lovable book'.

The 'sense of the man himself' counted for a good deal in his estimate of Keats. When Thomas was writing, the hey-day of Keats as the 'apostle of beauty' had passed, but he was still overwhelmingly and for many readers exclusively the dreamy and melancholy poet of sensuous impressions. Thomas, while praising the sensuousness wherever he feels it to be fresh and life-giving and not sickly, lays stress on the core of extraordinary strength and human sympathies in Keats. One of his warmest tributes to an author is his account of Keats's character. He sees the 'friendliness':

> When he writes a poem to a poet or stops in 'Endymion' to apologize to an old poet or old tale, it is with

a friendliness lacking in Milton's reference to Homer, or Wordsworth's to Milton, or Tennyson's to Wordsworth.

He finds that Keats's letters to his women friends and acquaintances

> suggest a comradeship, not deep, but frank and free, and almost equal, for which parallels are not easily found outside our own age.

He notes the 'adult cynical humour' in *Lamia*, and the firm masculine attitude, the 'more intellectual and assured tone'. He speaks of Keats's 'vivacity and judgment, and clear, determined thinking about man and nature'. He emphasizes qualities that even to-day are by no means generally recognized:

> For very long tracts of time Keats was one of the soberest, soundest, keenest, and most kindly brains that ever considered man and God.

He reminds us of Keats's interest in contemporary events, his concern for progress and improvement in human affairs:

> . . . in his last illness he wanted Cobbett to be elected to Parliament, and said: 'O that I had two double plumpers for him.'

He reminds us, too, that it was Keats who said: 'The sward is richer for the tread of a real nervous English foot.' Thomas values the humanity of Keats as he does that of Jefferies, the fine *human* nature that he has, and which glows out in the words he speaks for men to listen to. I think Thomas overestimates the 'Bright Star' sonnet; certainly he becomes over-eloquent about it. But the last remark in his account of it suggests the depth of both Keats's and his own regard for literature and for life:

The poem, for living men, adds a beauty to life and a new ground for desiring it.

Thomas is not a critic who formulates significant and memorable 'laws' or *dicta*, or one of those who express their finds in more or less brilliant phrasing. But he does often convey his insights with an admirable pointedness:

(Of Suckling): The cynical poems belong to his age, the serious to himself. They suggest a society where women were over-flattered and under-valued, and their sentiments are those which young men, probably in all ages, feel called upon to express in the convivial company of many equals and no friends.

Milton insists much upon the 'naked beauty' of Eve, 'undecked save with herself' and 'no veil she needed, virtue proof', and 'Eve ministered naked'. He is also fond of pointing out that she felt no 'dishonest shame', and that 'no thought inferior altered her cheek', that 'Love unlibidinous reigned', that she received Adam's courtship with 'innocence and virgin modesty'—phrases which seem to show that the opposite was in his mind, and at least have the effect of suggesting the opposite to the reader; the poet himself is, as it were, a seventeenth-century intruder upon the scene, and really gives some indecency to the nakedness.

(Of Milton again): . . . He also wrote five Italian sonnets and a canzone to an Italian lady, probably not Leonora, though she charmed him by her voice, as well as her grace and her black-eyed and dark-haired beauty. But sooner or later there must have come a certain awkwardness in regarding the physical side of women, if we may draw any conclusion from the slightly grotesque and monstrous impression made by Eve and in a lesser degree by Adam in 'Paradise Lost', as if they were half marble and half flesh, and in any case imperfectly visualized and resting too much upon the traditional or conventional view.

A man may some day arise who can understand Pope's 'Windsor Forest', and, getting behind its convention, see just what love of old trees it meant in Queen Anne's time. What must never be forgotten is that in any poem the traditional art element is the all but necessary medium for expressing any passion, whether simple and fleshly or hesitating and complicated.

Central matters in his authors are shrewdly pointed to, and the judgments are often in line with the findings of later notable critics, as when he speaks of Milton's confused treatment of love and of Adam and Eve, and of the same poet's 'imperfect visualization'. Moral discrimination is an essential part of the total assessment. 'Modern', too, is his comparison of Clare and Burns in *A Literary Pilgrim in England*. Clare is much enjoyed—'no one reads him but loves him'—for his 'fresh sweet spirituality' and his grasp of detail, but his lack of any great force is noted:

> Unlike Burns, he had practically no help from the poetry and music of his class. He was a peasant writing poetry, yet cannot be called a peasant poet, because he had behind him no tradition of peasant literature, but had to do what he could with the current forms of polite literature.

Later in the same book we have this:

> Burns's country was the Lowlands of Scotland. The poor, free peasantry culminated in him. Poetry does not sum up, but his poetry was the flower and the essence of that country and its peasantry. He was great because they were all at his back, their life and their literature.

If we had not known that Thomas was the author of these passages, with their emphasis on the relation of the writer to the culture within which he lives, we might easily have assigned them to our own time.

Thomas's ideas about such categories in literature as words, the order of words, rhythm, control of material, and so on, almost always occur as it were incidentally, when he is dealing with a particular writer or work. But though he is not a theorist in criticism he does, of course, sometimes generalize. Here he is stressing the need for self-sufficiency in a work of art:

> Whatever be the subject, the poem must not depend for its main effect upon anything outside itself except the humanity of the reader.

About the properties and effects of words and their ordering, he has obviously thought much. He writes of a Maeterlinck poem:

> The piece is hardly more than a catalogue of symbols that have no more literary value than words in a dictionary. It ignores the fact that no word, outside works of information, has any value beyond its surface value except what it receives from its neighbours and its position among them.

And there is an excellent page in *Walter Pater* that deals with a dead use of words, or a faulty use:

> 'Scholarship', says the Pateresque Lionel Johnson, 'is the only arbiter of style.' It may be so, and it may also be that scholarship will in the end convert posterity to 'gibbous towns'. In the meantime 'gibbous' remains a word not sufficiently full and exact to be of scientific value, and having no other value in this place, is but a label.

He goes on to say, in a passage that may recall certain key ideas of T. S. Eliot's criticism:

> No man can decree the value of one word, unless it is his own invention; the value which it will have in his hands has been decreed by his own past, by the past of

his race. It is, of course, impossible to study words too deeply, though all men are not born for this study.

The change, generally speaking, that has come over the quality and function of language—broadly, from concrete expressiveness to an abstract and perfunctory utilitarianism—was perceived and regretted by Thomas:

> Words are no longer symbols, and to say 'hill' or 'beech' is not to call up images of a hill or a beech-tree, since we have so long been in the habit of using the words for beautiful and mighty and noble things very much as a book-keeper uses figures without seeing gold and power. (*The South Country*)

It will be remembered that Yeats also hated the 'abstract'; he is like Thomas when he refers in his *Essays* to the 'impersonal language that has come, not out of individual life, nor out of life at all, but out of the necessities of commerce, of parliament, of board schools, of hurried journeys by rail', and when he says, 'One must not forget that the death of language, the substitution of phrases as nearly impersonal as algebra for words and rhythms varying from man to man, is but a part of the tyranny of impersonal things'.

But the most interesting parallels are with T. S. Eliot. We have already seen Thomas concerned (and concerned as a literary critic and not as literary historian) with certain questions that rise out of considering the writer in his relation to a tradition, and the approach suggested by the following remark, made in reference to Swinburne's *Bothwell*, would be appreciated by the later critic:

> For a nineteenth-century lyric poet, in an age without poetic drama, to revive a form early discarded by Elizabethan dramatists, was an adventure more grim than serious.

(Incidentally, it is characteristic that Thomas continues with a remark in which the positive appreciations, precisely because they are sincerely meant—'voice', 'character'—make the nicely balanced irony the more effective:

> That he read it aloud to his friends without causing any suffering that has yet become famous is a superb testimony to his voice, to his character, and to his friends.

The delightful sentence doesn't at all impair the seriousness of his general critical approach.)

Mr Eliot thinks in much the same way, and comes to the same conclusions, about Swinburne, as Thomas does. Thomas, after saying that there are too many words, inessential words, in Swinburne, and pointing out that 'their growth is by simple addition rather than evolution', asks 'Who would miss a couple of queens from the crowd of Herodias, Aholibah, Cleopatra . . .?' (he lists more than twenty), and then adds: 'Nevertheless the reader would not willingly consent to their disappearance.' Mr Eliot's way of saying much the same thing is this:

> His diffuseness is one of his glories. That so little material as appears to be employed in *The Triumph of Time* should release such an amazing number of words requires what there is no reason to call anything but genius. You could not condense *The Triumph of Time*. You could only leave out. And this would destroy the poem; though no one stanza seems essential.

Again, we have seen Thomas demonstrating the lack of the actual in Swinburne: 'Swinburne's style touches actual detail only at its peril'; and Mr Eliot states that in Swinburne's verse 'the object has ceased to exist'; both critics give examples of words in Swinburne that flourish with a life of their own and only with that life. But perhaps the plainest instance of this close similarity in critical think-

ing and comment comes with the examination of these
famous lines:

> Before the beginning of years
> There came to the making of man
> Time with a gift of tears;
> Grief with a glass that ran.

Both critics point to incongruities in the prose meaning
while admitting the power of the sound. Here is Thomas:

> This has that appearance of precision which Swinburne
> always affected, which is nothing but an appearance.
> . . . It may be that Time received the 'gift of tears' in-
> stead of the 'glass that ran' solely for the sake of allitera-
> tion. It would doubtless be better if it were not so, but
> nothing can be perfect from every point of view, and
> this deceitful deference to the pure intellect I speak of
> chiefly to show what Swinburne's use of the sounds and
> implications of words can overcome.

And here is Mr Eliot:

> This is not merely 'music'; it is effective because it
> appears to be a tremendous statement, like statements
> made in our dreams; when we wake up we find that the
> 'glass that ran' would do better for time than for grief,
> and that the gift of tears would be as appropriately
> bestowed by grief as by time.

One of Mr Eliot's most famous remarks is that which
concerns the impersonality of art:

> . . . the more perfect the artist, the more perfectly
> separated in him will be the man who suffers and the
> mind which creates; the more perfectly will the mind
> digest and transmute the passions which are its material.

In *Lafcadio Hearn* Thomas states that 'the personality of
the writer is in his best work shown by his abnegation of
personality'; and in a discussion of Keats's Odes he comes

even closer to Mr Eliot's thought: among his remarks on the 'Grecian Ode' is this: 'Its personality is submerged, and the more intense for that', and later we have:

> Thus in the odes the poet made for himself a form in which the essence of all his thought, feeling, and observation, could be stored without overflowing or disorder; of its sources in its daily life there was no more shown than made his poems quick instead of dead.

(I do not wish to suggest, by giving these instances, that an all-over comparison of Thomas and Mr Eliot as critics would be very valuable. But the resemblances in some directions are so interesting, and Thomas's virtues are so indisputable, that such a comparison would at least be possible and would not be at all grotesque.)

Order and control are qualities supremely valued by Thomas. He is careful to point out that the author of the Odes is also the author of *St Mark*, and says that in this poem Keats 'seems to have become entangled in visible things not sufficiently under control to be effective, except separately and one by one'. And of Pater's *Child in the House* he remarks: '... partly because his material was not clear and definite enough, his thoughts floated hither and thither.' These are but two examples from many.

He emphasizes the 'organic' quality of rhythm in writing, and though he admits the kind of hypnotic power that some incantatory rhythms have, he is quite definite about the need for a relationship to the spoken language if rhythm is to be richly expressive. He speaks more than once of 'the rhythms which only emotion can command'.

Normally, however, Thomas is not so exacting about rhythm, or at least does not write so much about it, as about staleness or confusion in thought and meaning, especially when they are accompanied with a superficial emotional effect. In the following passage it is interesting to see him using verbal analysis in touching (among other things) upon the question, so well-discussed in our time, of 'stock responses':

> The first line of *Hesperia*—
>> 'Out of the golden remote wild west where the sea
>>> without shore is',
> is an example of Swinburne's way of accumulating words which altogether can suggest rather than in-fallibly express his meaning. 'Golden', 'remote', 'wild', 'west', 'sea', and 'without shore' all have already some emotional values, of which the line gives no more than the sum, the rhythm and grammatical connection saving the words from death and inexpressiveness. In the whole opening passage of this poem there is the same accumulation, aided by the vague, as in 'region of stories' and 'capes of the past oversea'.

This scrupulousness in analysis is matched by a thoroughness in supplying instances to support his judg-ments, and by a concern for accuracy of fact. He can show what Swinburne takes in the way of rhyming habits, archaisms, Satanism, exuberance, and so on, from Rossetti, Morris, Baudelaire, Hugo, Malory, the Bible. He frequently compares two versions of a piece of writing and discusses the point of the changes made by the author. He suggests that in a certain Coleridge dictum a 'must' could with advantage be altered to a 'may'. He provides (in the book on Borrow) details of the activities of the Bible Society in Spain. Often he gives in detail the cir-cumstances of the composition of a work, and the author's environment and family affairs. The thoroughness is not always relevant for criticism; it is employed on inessentials as well as for significant illumination. Sometimes it is felt to be dictated by the need for the requisite number of pages to be filled, and we sense the weariness of his researches into material which he was not really interested in. But on balance the thoroughness serves him well; it is in the service of criticism.

Thomas never fails to say what he can for an author, however antipathetic his judgment on the whole may be. If he shows Swinburne's thinking to be vague, and his ardours to have something spurious about them, he also praises the energetic rhythms and the variety of his music; a typical comment is: 'The magnificence of the movement absorbs much flaw in the substance.' He is always aware of the shortcomings of Borrow as man and writer, but he pays his tribute, qualified though it is and often making its way through a deal of irony, as in the following:

> In these repressed indoor days, we like a swaggering man who does justice to the size of the planet. We run after biographies of extraordinary monarchs, poets, bandits, prostitutes, and see in them magnificent expansions of our fragmentary, undeveloped, or mistaken selves. . . . Borrow, as his books portray him, is admirably fitted to be our hero.

What he sees as good and valuable in Pater and Maeterlinck and others is always given full mention. Thomas is the opposite of niggardly. He can praise the slight, as when saying of Carew's 'Ask me no more': 'Such a poem shows how little need the lyric has of the best that is thought and said in the world. It is made of materials that are worth nothing and is itself yet beyond price.'

An article entitled 'On Reviewing, an Unskilled Labour', printed in *Poetry and Drama*, March 1914, is interesting both in its strong feeling and in the views offered, the criteria stated or implied:

> Most reviewers have no aim clearly before them, except of covering space and putting the name of the book at

the top. At best they want to get in a striking phrase, relevant or not. God help them.

The reviewer's own writing, Thomas says, may have the sort of interest that comes of reading Wilde's *Critic as Artist*, but it isn't criticism. He deplores the use of 'important-looking abstractions and generalities' and of degraded loose words and phrases such as 'unequalled', 'absolutely pure'. He finds the prevailing manner and tone faulty:

> Nearly all reviews of verse are either loosely complimentary or have a bantering tone as if the bards were tiny little odd unreal creatures who earn no wages and have no human feelings.

He wants an honest account of one's response to a book, and if that is found too difficult, then he believes that the beginnings of a 'skilled labour' might come from a plain, full, descriptive account of the book. He speaks of reviewers as 'a rabble of ridiculous and unlovely muddlers', and though it is mainly feeling that he is there expressing, he has by then said enough to justify his use of 'muddlers' and to show that it is muddle that he reasonably dislikes. The article is an expression of his concern for the function of criticism.

And yet, with such standards and with all his insight and intelligence, he sometimes surprises us with his judgments and preferences and with a manner and tone not in keeping with his aim of clear unambiguous utterance. The beauty of the melody of 'Greensleeves' draws him into a dream two pages long about the possible circumstances of its origin; he can say of a Swinburne poem: 'The rhyming words have a life of their own, as of birds singing or fauns dancing.' Such lapses into an appeal which is more or less emotive are not, however, frequent enough to count for

much in the whole. But considered preferences are a
different matter. There is, for instance, his excessive regard
for C. M. Doughty as the author of that interesting huge
curiosity, *The Dawn in Britain*: he speaks of Doughty's
'great, original and strange intellect', of the 'wonderful
brevity, precision, consistency, and power' of his style. He
is admittedly a little uneasy about 'a vocabulary and an
eccentricity so much outside the tradition of English
poetry', but the book 'does reincarnate and reinspire the
ancient life that was once lived in this land'. Thomas
states that in pity 'no English poet except Shakespeare
equals him'. We have to conclude that when he was
writing about *The Dawn in Britain* Thomas was unduly
affected by the vast amount of 'ancient English history' in
the poem, and didn't sufficiently separate the poet's intentions and the poem's achievement. And yet, paradoxi-
cal as it may seem, we feel that Thomas would have had
no difficulty in contrasting this poem with *Sir Gawain and
the Green Knight* (which obviously must have moved and
delighted him if he ever read it).

Meredith also, it seems to me, is overpraised; the 'love
of earth', the vigour and the sensuousness, are not there
in his writing to the extent that Thomas states (in *In
Pursuit of Spring*; it is fair to add that later, in *A Literary
Pilgrim in England*, he is more critical, but though he shows
he doesn't care for the element of abstract principle in
Meredith's nature-loving—'A walk for him is an intellectual thing. He enjoys it, but knows also that it is good
for him, body and soul'—he still isn't so severe as we
might have expected him to be on the over-writing and
the gesturing). Again, while it is wholly good and right
that Thomas should emphasize Hudson's distinction as
a naturalist, is Hudson's writing, except perhaps at oc-
casional moments, of such quality as to make us feel that

he presents 'the substantial miracle of a naturalist and an imaginative artist in one and in harmony'?

It is Hudson who says, in the foreword to *Cloud Castle*, that Thomas was intolerant of inferior verse, and in his heart he unquestionably was. But his 'kindness', especially with contemporary poets, often impeded the free expression of his judgment. A lot of very minor poets get much more commendation from Thomas than they should have. We may be right in seeing in the following remark a touch of uneasiness caused by his inclination to be unduly generous: 'Abercrombie, I fancy, applies the lash, and I wonder whether he always did. I used to think he was naturally a spirited steed. I am always anxious to like him.' Kindness, however, has its limits, and unequivocally adverse judgments are given sometimes. Flecker, for instance, is 'one of the artificers in verse that I can't get on with, the decorators, like Wilde, who carry Keats's style to its logical extreme without genius'. Bad anthologies, mere book-making, are strongly attacked: of one he says, 'The whole thing is either a joke or a shameless commercial enterprise'; of another, '. . . does not reveal any authority, skill, or novel idea'; of a third, 'They do not give all the poems written about birds and butterflies, nor the best ones, nor representative ones, but simply any ones'.

Ezra Pound, for Thomas, was certainly not one of the 'decorators'. A review of *Personae* (1909) shows that he perceived the interesting 'new' voice, a voice with many faults, however: old and foreign words with too abstruse a meaning, tricky inverted commas, rhythms that are now too free and now too stiff, 'gobbets of Browningesque', bad construction 'which we cannot unravel and are inclined to put down as not the only case of imperfect correction of proofs'. Nevertheless, Thomas finds, pointing out his own seeming paradox, that 'the chief part of his power is directness and simplicity', and stresses the 'personality' of Pound as Mr Eliot was to stress it in his Introduction to the *Selected Poems* in 1928. That he felt keenly the force of the unusual poetry is further shown by the rather curious conclusion of the review, where, though we are likely to think that he need not have felt so humble in the presence of the author of *Personae*, he does well in stating his sense of the lack of any powerful critical tradition or movement in his day: he says he would like to 'apologize to him [i.e. the poet] for our shortcomings and to any other readers for that insecurity of modern criticism of which we feel ourselves at once a victim and a humble cause'. And, indeed, it was a poor period for criticism. Thomas might well have looked round for someone who since the death of Arnold or perhaps of Leslie Stephen could as critic win his full admiration.

There were factors (apart from the question of penchant or drive) that worked against Edward Thomas's achieving the unremitting exercise of insight, the sustained rigour, that mark the great critic, a rigour of applied intelligence that can be apparent in incidental utterances as well as in full works. Nevertheless, one would have thought that his critical writings and comments supply evidence of a mind interesting and keen enough to gain him considerable respect as a critic. Many of his admirers still seem hardly to know that he wrote any literary criticism, and some of them, having apparently read it, have quite failed to appreciate its qualities. One can understand anyone saying: 'There are a lot of books to read, life is short, and I can't be interested any more in Walter Pater.' But it is hard to understand how anyone who is interested in Thomas, and who has read his book on Pater, can say, as Mr Moore does: 'Edward's *Pater* ... has an air of having

been written in a spacious library during short spells after
dinner between sips of port.' Apart from the fact that the
Pater has behind it a deal of solid work and in it much acute
thinking and evaluation of the kind that shows Thomas's
intense interest in life and literature (however much of a
'task' he may have felt the writing of the book to be), it
must come from a very odd notion of Thomas as a whole
that he can be thought capable of the sort of writing suggested by that 'sips of port' quotation. Certainly he loved
all the old drinking songs, and he relished, as keenly as
anybody could, what there was left of life in the 'old inns of
England'; but his love of 'easy hours' did not at all involve
a shallowness. 'Incapable of insincerity in any ordinary
sense', F. R. Leavis has said of him.

The following passage occurs near the end of the book
on Jefferies:

> Nothing is more mysterious than this power [i.e. of
> using words], along with the kindred powers of artist
> and musician. It is the supreme proof, above beauty,
> physical strength, intelligence, that a man or woman
> lives. Lighter than gossamer, words can entangle and
> hold fast all that is loveliest, and strongest, and fleetest,
> and most enduring, in heaven and earth. They are for
> the moment, perhaps, excelled by the might of policy
> or beauty, but only for the moment, and then all has
> passed away; but the words remain, and though they
> also pass away under the smiling of the stars, they mark
> our utmost achievement in time.

The slight intrusion of the 'personal' felt here in the
introduction of gossamers and stars (an implied juxtaposition, by the way, profoundly characteristic of Thomas),
doesn't interfere with the general tone and import, and
I think no one is likely to question the force and sincerity
of the impelling interests. And though there are in

Thomas's criticism irrelevancies, lapses due to specialist enthusiasms and to 'kindness' and to relaxed attention, and though it can be diffuse and repetitive, it is the work of a man who thought and felt for himself, who based his judgments, as all critics ultimately must, on his own carefully considered experience, who approached literature in a spirit never dilettante and never piously solemn, and who endeavoured to give his findings clear and exact expression.

Perhaps it would be as well to say that when it was earlier stated that a comparison between Thomas and Mr Eliot would not be grotesque, it was not intended to suggest that the critical stature of the two writers is the same. Critical work was a more peripheral activity for Thomas than it has been for Mr Eliot; he did not *develop* his sensibility towards that end, so that the work achieved is not of the scope and power that could have effected a reorientation even if it had been better known. Nevertheless, it belongs unquestionably to the minority stream of criticism which, powered by Arnold and to a lesser degree by Leslie Stephen and certain writers in *Blackwood's*, the *Edinburgh*, *Fraser's*, etc., continued the central though minority tradition in opposing those Victorian sentiments and tendencies which had the effect of belittling literature even while solemnly acclaiming it. The mind displayed in Thomas's criticism is of the kind and quality that demands the sort of respect that we accord to our finest critics; and the criticism itself is remarkably like some of the aspects of the best criticism of our own day, in its methods as well as in its assumptions and preoccupations.

CHAPTER FIVE

Character and Temperament.
The Cloud

IN our attempt to come to a satisfying understanding of the character and temperament of a writer we have not known personally, there is inevitably an area where we depend on others and where what they have said or written witnesses to a truth and an experience which it would be presumptuous to think we can improve upon. For instance, Helen Thomas's book—or two books in one —gives us an incomparably vivid impression of the man she knew for the greater part of his life. In its vitality, its good sense, its frankness, its final pathos, it is irreplaceable as a record and indispensable to everyone who is interested in Edward Thomas. One's reason for attempting to add to what it provides is that the writings uncover things not explicit and sometimes not even discernible in the activities of living, and that some interesting judgments and opinions have been given by others who knew him. Possibly this chapter would not have been written at all if the 'mysterious' melancholy were not so generally associated with him.

An account of Thomas's character and temperament, given in simple terms and on the evidence of his everyday relations with people, would lay the chief stress, I think, on these qualities: the quiet and reserve that go with contemplativeness, a deep self-distrust, a recurring and never finally explicable melancholia; but with the reserve, the self-distrust, the melancholy, a personal kindliness and loyalty, a sympathy with suffering, a sense of humour, a capacity for joy in beauty, and, above all, a sincerity which showed itself in his dealing and manner with people and in his approach to his writing. It is probable that when Helen refers to his 'strange, complex temperament', it is the disturbing, seemingly unmotivated changes of mood that she has most in mind. 'You must not therefore expect me to say anything outright. It is not my way, is it?' he wrote to her in a war letter. The reticence, about which he was always debating with himself, made it the more difficult for his acquaintances to feel sure they 'knew' him. And for some of them the difficulty was increased by their apparent inability to recognize the sincerity of a man struggling to remain a living individual person, and setting high value on the beauty of the fresh natural world, in an age organized more and more for commercial and industrial ends.

To Hudson, Thomas was primarily a mystic; the emphasis here is on the contemplative. Thomas Seccombe saw him as 'fundamentally a humorist'. E. S. P. Haynes speaks of his 'inveterate shyness' and of his lack of 'push and go', while also praising his talk (in Oxford days) as 'incomparable'. Edward Garnett similarly speaks of his 'shy diffidence', but also says, 'most masculine in his independence, never swerving in his proud, self-contained attitude'. Norman Douglas deplores what he considers his aloofness and ultra-refinement, and gives it as his opinion that Thomas would have been the better for a 'little touch of bestiality'. Mr de la Mare, on the other hand, in his loving and generous Foreword to the *Collected Poems*, sees the refinement as the index of 'his compassionate and suffering heart, his fine, lucid, grave, and sensitive mind', and leaves us in no doubt as to the impact made on him by

Thomas's personality. To Mrs Conrad he appeared 'the quintessence of gentleness', and though Helen could have modified that view for the wife of the great novelist, an extraordinary gentleness was in fact a part of the 'strange, complex temperament'. Mr J. W. Haines, a close friend during Thomas's last years, sees him essentially, as Hudson does, as a 'contemplative'; he has also told me that on all the occasions when they walked and talked together Thomas was never in the 'dark' mood.

It may be profitable to explore a little in certain other directions before we come to consider the author of the poems, who is and is not the Thomas of these prose chapters.

We have seen how his deep awareness of a certain aspect of nature could give rise to a feeling—a feeling and a condition, not an idea or a conclusion merely—of his insubstantiality in the world. When he was trying to escape from that strange dawn harmony of 'bird, wind, and man', it was his identity as a *human* being that he felt to be in danger of dissolving into a vast and incomprehensible universe. There is also the always-recurring silence, an awareness of which is likely to be anything but an encouragement or a support to confident thoughts of human powers and potentialities:

> But as we reached the stile our tongues and our steps ceased together, and I was instantly aware of the silence through which our walking and talking had drawn a thin line up to this point. (*Light and Twilight*)

And in the city also, the undifferentiated tumult may become for him a kind of silence in which human meaning is lost:

> The roar in which all played a part developed into a kind of silence which not any of these millions could

break; the sea does not absorb the little rivers more completely than this silence the voices of men and women, than this solitude their personalities.

(*The South Country*)

In a very early essay he comes to a castle 'as if upon time itself', time which has been 'overtaken by eternity', for the masonry is now indistinguishable from the rock. And often the manifestation of the individual life seems to him thin and ineffectual in the confused (though harmonious), powerful circumambience which is the reality:

... the song of the missel thrush that came through the storm like a mere ode to liberty in the midst of revolution. (*The Heart of England*)

If this way of perceiving had been so exclusive in Thomas as to make for mere negativeness and despair, he would have been, of course, a much less interesting man and writer. But even when he was 'sadly' conscious of the transience of the actual, conscious of the 'reverberation' of hollowness, he could joy, like Keats, in the power of the imagination to give a lasting life to things; as here, in *The Heart of England*, where an old man is bringing the cows slowly along a curving road for the afternoon milking:

They turn under the archway of a ruined abbey, and low as if they enjoy the reverberation, and disappear. I never see them again; but the ease, the remoteness, the colour of the red cattle in the green road, the slowness of the old cowman, the timelessness of that gradual movement under the fourteenth-century arch, never vanish.

And even when, in *Wales*, a thick mist causes him to feel that the world is gone 'like last year's clouds', yet 'strangely sufficient was the mist, the hard road, and the moist stick in my hand'.

Sometimes his sense of the non-human quality in

humanity itself was disturbingly acute. In the course of describing some Cornishwomen types in *The South Country*, he remarks, 'The eyes of most human beings are causes of bewilderment and dismay if curiously looked at', and he goes on to describe those of an old Cornishwoman, round and black and with a 'cold brightness . . . like a stone':

> Such intense loneliness and strangeness did they create, since they proclaimed shrilly and clearly that beyond a desire to be fed and clothed we had nothing in common.

This way of apprehending, with its implications for human relationships, was not habitual and overpowering in Thomas—one imagines it would lead to madness in anyone in whom it was so—but it was sharp enough to increase his general and on the whole disconcerting feeling that man is at least as much a creature on the face of the earth as he is a human being. In *The Heart of England*, the old woman whom he calls Margaret Helen Page is to him a proof that

> man is older than Christ and Buddha, than Jehovah and Jupiter, and that not even such presences on the earth have left behind footprints in which he can wander with security.

She is in a sense religious and a Christian, but Thomas sees her acts and her language as revealing essentially 'the multitude's eternal paganism, which religions ruffle and sink into again'.

Such a sense of the eternal and the unchanging may lead to explicit statements like the following:

> How little do we know of the business of the earth, not to speak of the universe; of time, not to speak of eternity. It was not by taking thought that man survived the mastodon. The acts and thoughts that will

serve the race, that will profit this commonwealth of things that live in the sun, the air, the earth, the sea, now and through all time, are not known and never will be known. The rumour of much toil and scheming and triumph may never reach the stars, and what we value not at all, are not conscious of, may break the surface of eternity with endless ripples of good. We know not by what we survive. . . . We can do the work of the universe though we shed friends and country and house and clothes and flesh, and become invisible to mortal eyes and microscopes. We do it now invisibly, and it is not these things which are us at all.

(*The South Country*)

We are not here concerned with discussing the desirability or otherwise of such a philosophy, beyond saying—what is perhaps obvious—that this kind of scepticism is not in the least the same thing as the futility-of-life brand of pessimism: the tone in which our littleness or lack of sure knowledge is averred is not cynical. What we have to stress at this point is that the man who wrote those words was not likely to have much confidence in any formulated codes of behaviour for men or in any organized activities for the promotion of happiness and virtue. We aren't at all surprised by Thomas's 'confession' that he cannot grasp politics, science, racing, the drama, book-clubs, nor when he says that although he finds many pleasures in cathedrals, 'they are incomprehensible and not restful. I feel when I am within them that I know why a dog bays at the moon'. He likes the avenue of archaic bossy lime trees that leads to the cathedral better than the cathedral itself.

It may have been that his sense of not being able to belong securely to any group sharpened and deepened his consciousness of the 'other' in nature, making it loom the larger and so adding to the difficulty of adjustment in the human scheme of things. Or it may have been that the

sense of the other was deep and inherent in his consciousness from the first, and so made it enormously difficult for
him to have any feeling of human solidarity. Whether we
choose one of these explanations, or whether we opt firmly
for a combination of the innate and the environmental, we
are always aware of a certain feeling of isolation as being
at the heart of Thomas's melancholy. He speaks frequently himself about isolation; a characteristic passage is
this from a letter to Gordon Bottomley in 1904:

> All my life I have been in the hands of those who care
> for other and even opposite things; and they have tried
> to teach me—or by my own imitative nature I have
> tried to learn—to say much and smartly about things I
> care nothing for. . . . Work that depends always and
> entirely upon a man's own invention and impulse always
> lets the artist down into deep waters of misery now and
> then, and at those times I have sought the company of
> many and various men, and yet I have always been
> alone and unaided; all I have got from them has been
> experiences which I never use. I have talked my soul
> empty to a man who (as I had not the wit to discover)
> answered me with his tongue; not one man but a
> score: I suppose, as I hinted just now, that my talk was
> obscure. . . . I think, for the mere health of the brain, a
> variety of social intercourse should be good: and I wish
> you were able to try it. But with me, social intercourse
> is only an intense form of solitude, and as solitude is
> what I have to avoid, the means are yet to be found. . . .
> I am glad you like 'the rapture of the fight'. I hardly
> ever do.

Being in the hands of 'those who care for other and
even opposite things' had long been a source of unease to
Thomas. One of the main impressions that we carry away
from his autobiography of childhood and boyhood is that
of his misery in certain situations. Although, as he tells us,

he and his father—his parents were, he says, 'sober reverent people without a creed'—made merry about the Devil and Hell, his dislike of chapel had little enough of merriment in it, the chapel where—

> from the prickly silence of two hundred or three hundred people I gradually came to feel a mild poison steadily creeping into me on all sides;

and when chapel was over—

> the deathly solemnity was strong enough to cling about the people even there in the sunlight: some of them it accompanied to their one o'clock roast beef and mutton.

As he grew up he began to hate the Sunday streets and his stiff Sunday clothes and 'everything that seemed a circling part of that deathly solemnity as I was not', and there developed a 'profound quiet detestation of Sunday' which was never to leave him. He liked hymns such as 'Jerusalem the Golden' and 'Fair waved the golden corn' (compare Lawrence's essay, 'Hymns in a Man's Life': *Phoenix*), but the teachings were 'airy nothings' to him, and 'Our Father' 'was and has ever remained Greek to me'. At St Paul's School he was often wretched and lonely; he did not talk much: 'What I did say I often felt to be obscure or false, but for fear of worse I did not correct it.' He was shy and frightened of encountering people in shops, and of distant relatives, and of grown-ups, who all seemed to him bold and confident.

As told in the sober and steady tone of *The Childhood of Edward Thomas*, we accept these things and many more like them as important in retrospect to the grown man. The evidence is sound, the childhood not falsified, and probably coloured only in the smallest degree by the adult's predilections. But we should be on our guard against making too much of it, or of such a factor as his 'conflict' with his father, in our consideration of his mature character. The miseries, the dislikes and loathings, the feeling of being opposed or 'out of it', must, of course, have been formative influences, but so they are in a myriad lives which we are content in our complacency to accept as normal. Moreover, the same book shows a boy with his tops and marbles, his fishing and cowboys and 'Urkey' and fly the garter, and a boy with a fondness for the girls which he says was of the serious and not the flirtatious kind. I do not myself believe that it was the external circumstances of his childhood that were responsible for such an unequivocal statement as this (from *The Heart of England*):

> It is a commonplace that each one of us is alone, that every piece of ground where a man stands is a desert island with footprints of unknown creatures all round its shore;

or that brought about a condition of which the Guru's words to Hari (in L. H. Myers's *The Pool of Vishnu*) may be taken as a diagnosis: 'Your true self is living too much alone. That would account, partly, for the attacks of anguish from which you suffer.'

The Guru's words are, of course, widely applicable, and it is the *character* of the 'anguish' that makes Thomas's case remarkable, together with his attempts at analysing it. He was perfectly aware that the 'true self', the self with the deep-lying impulses and desires, the real as opposed to the social self—ideally there is no antithesis—suffers when these impulses and desires have for whatever reason to remain hidden from others and to remain unfulfilled. But for most of his life he was uncertain, and allowed himself to be perplexed by his uncertainty, as to what his true self was. This condition is not uncommon either. What is unusual in Thomas's case is the force and persistence of the dissatisfaction and the worrying about himself. His prose writings have numerous characters who either in themselves or by way of an encounter actual or imagined with the narrator are devices for self-analysis.

The man Hawthornden (in *Light and Twilight*) is clearly, in essentials, a self-portrait, and we note in the account the pervasive self-distrustful tone as well as what is explicitly stated; and where Hawthornden isn't exactly Thomas he is what Thomas fears he may become. Hawthornden half withdraws from life, reading many books and becoming stiffened and chilled in his human relationships; he likes particularly the poetry of passion but feels that he is becoming less and less capable of passion himself and that he is living in a 'dim-pinnacled citadel of unreality'; it is difficult for him to live happily with his wife and children; he likes gypsies and tramps, and waits by roadsides and in taprooms for satisfying encounters, 'but something always stood in the way—himself'; sometimes when he saw a man he was interested in, he 'formed romantic conjectures which made him impatient of what he actually heard'; he would try to get nearer to the heart of a wayfarer by dressing negligently, but his efforts always failed, and when his wife told him that he couldn't disguise himself and that anyone could see what he really was, 'he liked the flattery, and remained discontented'; he liked tea and cakes and was fastidious about their quality, but he grew to dislike and reproach himself as 'the man who was always home to tea'. One afternoon Hawthornden fails to come in to tea; his heart has given out while he is running home: 'He had not only not come home to tea, but had ceased to think about tea, so far as can be known. He was dead.' Almost everything in this short essay shows an Edward Thomas dissatisfied with the man he saw himself to be.

Another of Thomas's 'other selves' is the 'lean indefinite man' whom he meets at the end of a day (in *The Icknield Way*) when 'the birds coming home to the quiet earth seemed visitors from another world'. This man cannot decide what happiness and unhappiness are; the day before this he had been digging clay and he had thought and thought 'till his brain could do nothing but remain aware of dull misery and the violent shocks of the hard work'; when night had come, 'the quiet, the magnitude of space, the noble lines of the range a little strengthened his spirit', but 'no thing or person in the world or out of it came into his mind with any conscious delight'. This man feels himself to be different from mature men,

> not by anything positive that could be called youth, but only by some undefinable lack which condemned him to a kind of overblown maturity. Thus when he consciously or unconsciously demanded a concession such as might be due to youth for some act or attitude, he met, in the individual or in society in some corporate form or other, a blankness or positive severity at which he recoiled with open but as yet uncertainly comprehending eyes.

He goes on to say that he is sometimes jealous of young men, and afraid of the middle-aged whom he had previously treated with some 'contempt or pitiful kindness'. He is jealous of his contemporaries though he has outstripped many of them in the race. Only towards one or two people has he

> a fair and easy freedom, and that only intermittently . . . therefore no more destitute and solitary man looked that night on the stars.

The context of this episode of the digging and thinking man turns out to be a romantic one: a woman's fresh strong voice is heard singing easily and joyously, and the writer breaks out with, 'Oh, for a horse to ride furiously, for a ship to sail . . . for a poet's pen!' But what the man has said is undoubtedly what Thomas thinks or suspects to be true of himself. The self-censure is, of course, excessive through self-mistrust.

The encounter with the Watercress Man in *The Heart of England* exhibits intentionally a divided Thomas. The old man carries a basket of wild flowers on his back; he is a painter of landscapes which suggest a Golden Age of beauty; he quotes glowingly from 'the one living pastoral poet' (Charles Dalmon, of whom Thomas was fond). But the narrator's response is hesitant, despite a rather brusque ironic note: 'I know nothing of literature. I am a journalist'; and later he 'stammers' out:

> Your aims are wonderful. If I could only see you at work, if you would only show me the scenes which inspire such antique and lofty emotions.

The irony is directed half against the old man for his suggested idealization and half against himself for his doubts.

Thomas's thinking (and 'worrying') was a good deal occupied with the incompatibility of an imagined ideal and the actual, and with kindred ideas or problems such as the difficulty of deciding between the claims of the contemplative-imaginative life and those of the life of everyday. Morgan Rhys, in *Wales*, is an idealist—' "If only we could think like that!" he said once, pointing to a fair, straight hawthorn that stood, with few branches and without leaves, on the mountain side'—but he has failed to achieve happiness,

> and so he tried to fortify himself by mingling warmly with the life of everyday in the village, where his

reputation was for generosity, hard drinking, and perfect latitude of speech.

He finds that he cannot live both lives. He begins to shrink away from men and outward experience and to 'live, as only too easily he could, upon his own fantasy'. And though he still advocates certain humane measures and gives his support to certain enthusiasms in the world of men, he now finds much enjoyment in silence and darkness, and in refraining from action, and he 'longed even to embrace the absolute blank of death, if only he could be just conscious of it'. He envies a preacher from the north who is forthright and passionate in his beliefs.

But amid all this perplexity of searching—a perplexity, as it appears in the prose, of pondering and meditation rather than of sharp, felt immediacy—there is always likely to appear a gleam of quiet humour. That same troubled Morgan Rhys describes a spring day on which he had felt a Wordsworthian blessedness and a perfection of harmony between the mazes of human activity and the clouds and hills and waters. His hearers are in great joy listening to him,

> though not without . . . a fear that he would spoil it by something inapposite. But merely remarking that he had seen the parson feeding his boar and that the harmony between them also was complete, he became silent. . . .

The innuendo is contained beautifully in the unemphatic manner—'merely remarking'—and whatever points of comparison we make for ourselves between parson and boar, the effect is the same: the harmony, on such a day, is real and a blessed one, while at the same time the elements that compose it are ironically equated and we have bathos. Parsons ought to smile at it.

Thomas does this sort of thing with a pleasant ease, and though he can be laboured and facetious it was again an excess of self-censure that made him write to Gordon Bottomley in 1902 (when he was twenty-four):

> True, I haven't violence. The nearest approach to it is the sham humour which I insert in order to make it clear that my feeble seriousness is as ridiculous to me as to others. I shall not fight against it.

It was to the same man that he wrote four years later:

> Such consistent people nearly always annoy me who am destined to reflect so many characters and to be none. What a barber was lost in me!

His humour is certainly not of the broad ebullient kind. Most often perhaps it rises out of a recognition of absurdity or pretentiousness or hypocrisy, and finds its expression in irony. Sometimes he is easily and tolerantly ironical:

> Little is known of Skelton, though very much was rumoured, and he became a ribald mythical character for two centuries; but it appears that when he was a parson at Diss he lived in comfortable concubinage with a woman whom he made the mother of many children and afterwards his wife.

And sometimes, as we have seen, he is angry, mocking, and bitter. In a letter to Hudson he said, '. . . the little humour I may have being inessential and unconsciously assumed as a weapon of defence'. Without discussing what essential humour is, or the degree in which most kinds of humour are defensive, we are likely to feel again that Thomas is being needlessly self-deprecating.

In more than one place Thomas is ironical about the self-satisfied dejection of 'the Celt', and about 'writer's melancholy' with its appearance of profundity. The frequency of these allusions is some measure of his introspection, but though they may be written down as defensive, they are not unconsciously so. He is quite aware of the extremity of his self-consciousness and is dissatisfied with it. At twenty-eight he writes: 'My self-criticism or rather my studied self-contempt is now nearly a disease.' Perhaps the most powerful direct expression of this particular dissatisfaction is in a letter written to Eleanor Farjeon in 1913; it is a very fine letter and must be given almost entire:

I don't want postcards from you except that they would put me at my ease, especially in these days when to write more than a page means attempting the impossible and wearying myself and uselessly afflicting others with some part of my little yet endless tale. It has got to its dullest and its worst page now. The point is I have got to help myself and I have been steadily spoiling myself for the job for I don't know how long. I am very incontinent to say these things. If I had never said them to anyone I should have been someone else and somewhere else. You see the central evil is self-consciousness carried as far beyond selfishness as selfishness is beyond self-denial (not very scientific comparison), and now amounting to a disease and all I have got to fight it with is the knowledge that in truth I am not the isolated self-considering brain which I have come to seem—the KNOWLEDGE that I am something more, but not the BELIEF that I can reopen the connection between that brain and the rest. I think perhaps having said that much I ought to say Don't speak to me about it, because it is endless and no good is to be done by talking or writing about it. And yet I am letting this go. Well, all my thoughts are by myself, alas. . . . And I keep afflicting myself by imagining all the distasteful work as if it were a great impassable mountain just

> ahead. Please forgive me and try not to give any
> thought to this flat grey shore which surprises the tide
> by being inaccessible to it.

The sharp distress recorded here comes from his knowledge
of the inadequacy of considering himself as an 'isolated
self-considering brain', and from his realizing that such
knowledge is useless. It is useless because he cannot create
for himself a *belief* in the possibility of wholeness, of an
integration of intellect, senses, instincts. Lawrence may
here be invoked again, with his insistence on the utter
necessity for us of re-establishing a nourishing relationship
with the 'cosmos': 'I am part of the great whole, and I can
never escape. But I *can* deny my connections, break them,
and become a fragment. Then I am wretched' (*Apocalypse*).
Thomas knows his wretchedness to come largely from his
'fragmentariness', from his denying of connections, and he
cannot find the faith to hope, as Lawrence never gave up
hoping to 're-establish the living organic connections with
the cosmos, the sun and earth, with mankind and nation
and family'. Thomas's relation with at least the sun and
the earth was a beautiful and life-giving one; but it was
not enough to save him from feeling, often, 'inaccessible
to the tide'. He deplored the 'pallid vice of reserve' which
he read in the faces of people, especially in city crowds, and
he disliked himself for not being immune from it. And he
fully knew the dangers of cultivating a 'sensibility' in
aloofness from the actualities of living.

In *The Heart of England* he more or less defines happiness
as 'unthwarted intensity of sensual and mental life, in the
midst of beautiful or astonishing things which should give
that life full play and banish expectation and recollection'.
The Heart of England first appeared in 1906, and Thomas
had eleven more years to live. But though he was to
develop and grow into the artist of the poems, I am not

sure that he would have given a very different prose definition of happiness in the years just before 1917, if he had then been concerned with that sort of thing. The poetry *is* concerned, of course, with the nature of happiness, and contains much that may remind us of a question he asked in that same early book: 'Is it perhaps true that those are never happy who know what happiness is?' And when he hears the lark singing 'high and wise things', he feels that there in the sky *is* the 'new joy of the spring . . . not asking to be understood but to be shared'. The references to self-consciousness are many and varied. 'Oh, my self-consciousness,' he writes miserably to Bottomley in 1907, 'it grows and grows and is almost constant now, and I fear perhaps it will reach the point of excess without my knowing it.' In *Wales* he writes: 'Sometimes, as when I passed Llanddeusant and Myddfai, I could see nothing that was there, because I was thinking of what had been long ago'; and he feels himself a 'wraith' whenever he encounters hard-working countrymen. One of the 'Thomas' characters in *The South Country* says:

As for myself, I am world-conscious, and hence suffer unutterable loneliness. I know what bitterness it is to be lacking in those strong tastes and impulses which, blinding men to what does not concern them, enable them to live with a high heart.

The tendency to idealize the lives of the 'unthinking' comes, of course, from the distress or regret at what he saw as an inability to share and to *be* more fully in life. We can be glad that he was to live to know that without his 'thinking', his troubling self-consciousness, the poetry could not have come into being.

In addition to this isolating and thwarting 'world-consciousness', there is the recurrent stated feeling of social man's extremely difficult and even anomalous place in the universe. This passage is characteristic:

> . . . all the joys of life that come through the nostrils from the dark, not understood world which is unbolted for us by the delicate and savage fragrances of leaf and flower and grass and clod, of the plumage of birds and fur of animals and breath and hair of women and children. How can our thoughts, the movements of our bodies, our human kindnesses, ever fit themselves with this blithe world? (*The South Country*)

(If the quotation had been at greater length, the word 'blithe' would not have appeared so odd as it does here, for Thomas has been indicating not only this 'dark, not understood world' but also the endless variety of shape and light and movement in nature. However, the main drift of the passage quoted is quite clear.)

At the root of the dark mood, then, in Edward Thomas —and it is fitting to repeat at this point that it was not by any means continuous—was a sharp sense of isolation, isolation as a human being in a non-human and ever-lasting universe, and isolation in the world of social men. As an artist, too, and as an idealist in so far as he perceived, like Jefferies, the immense potentialities of mankind (though ineluctably 'mortal'), he was aware of the weight and extent of the opposing forces. He must have learned to know, as much as anyone, the penalties attaching to sincerity in a world bountiful in deceits and evasions either trivial or monstrous. Then there were the domestic troubles, financial and otherwise—laid bare by Helen with an admirable frankness—and the drudgery involved in much of the commissioned prose writing, a drudgery the heavier because he was so conscientious, almost fearfully and morbidly so at times; there were tasks he could have skipped without any harm to his essential sincerity.

His dissatisfaction with much of his work must have made him feel the less at home in the world and the less wanted. Possibly if he had started writing poetry fifteen or twenty years earlier he would have found in his creativeness a victory over the 'cloud'. But it is only a possibility. The man whose characteristic (and oppressive) feeling about the racing crowd at Goodwood was that they 'had nothing in common but internal solitude and external pursuit of pleasure', who 'tried to console himself' now with the silences and spaces of the sky and now with the light and warmth and fellowship of the inn, was not fated to reach without more than usual difficulty the state we rather vaguely call fulfilment or serenity.

Many critics and others have given their opinion that 'all was well' with Thomas once he was in the army and leading what they call an active life. This opinion is to me staggering in its naïvety. It is true that he is 'cheerful' in many of his letters: he told Frost that he could obey and be happy; he wrote to his aunt that he had 'never been happier nor in better health'; 'I don't worry', he said. And, of course, he did his work well: his commanding officer wrote to Helen after his death that he was 'ready to do any job that was going with the same steadfast, unassuming spirit'. But it is fairly obvious that what Thomas found in escaping from civilian life was relief, and to say this is to indicate a weakness rather than a strength. In proportion as the relief was great, he was losing not finding himself. The self-consciousness might tend to diminish with his participation in work and activities that pertained to the world 'outside himself', but it is anything but a tribute to Thomas, with that sincerity and steadiness and insight, to suggest that he found himself by joining in with everybody else in that particular manifestation of civilized man's purpose and destiny. In the folly of democratic idealism the person of extraordinary fineness can be seen fulfilling himself in the firing of guns. An odd vision, and one would like to know what feelings and thoughts would be Edward Thomas's if he could walk now through 'the torn fields of France' at Arras and elsewhere. That the new activity might have led to a development of his character and powers is quite possible; nor do we forget that he enlisted because he 'loved England'. But there is nothing in his poetry that conveys the kind of tragic view of humanity's lot in war that, say, Rosenberg's poetry sometimes expresses. Nor has he any of the attitudes—how could he have?—of the conventional patriot:

> Beside my hate of one fat patriot
> My hatred of the Kaiser is love true.

In *World Without End* Helen gave the hint which should have made the all-was-well-from-then-on people think again: in the army, she says, 'his own inner life was submerged. . . .'

Thomas's nature was antithetical to the spirit of what I have called 'democratic idealism', to the tendencies represented by the watchwords and slogans that apparently are necessary to the conduct of wars and other mass-activities; he detested clap-trap, in any form and in any place. Writing about war poetry in *Poetry and Drama* (December, 1914), he says that the public 'want something raw and solid, or vague and lofty and sentimental. They must have Mr Begbie to express their thoughts, or "Tipperary" to drown them.' He states that most newspapers have someone who can 'take the easy words of a statesman' and dish them up loftily and thrillingly. He finds Chesterton's *Hymn of War* 'archaic and Hebraic', and he holds aloof, adding: 'They revert, and they may be right, though I cannot follow them if I would.' An abundance of instances in the *Marlborough* (1915) show not only how completely without illusions he was as to the glory of past battles and armies, but also that he took every opportunity to make his attitude clear: red and blue coats were 'no armour against rain, bullet, or lash', and 'prisoners must often have wished that they had fallen into the hands of God than of men', and so on. I believe it is more likely to have been utter despair than anything else that made Thomas want to leave his English camp and get to the front in France. Helen has this to say:

> David had been in the army a year. He hated it all—the stupidity, the injustice, the red tape, and the conditions of camp life. But he worked hard to perfect himself in the job he had undertaken to become a proficient soldier. (*World Without End*)

It would be interesting to discuss the state of mind of a man who carried in his pocket a copy of *Cymbeline* and the *Infantry Training Manual*.

In his letters of the war period there is much of the same doubting and self-distrust as formerly: '. . . if your love can help me, I shall be well, though what is well, who knows?' and more directly, 'I keep feeling I should enjoy it more if I knew I should survive it'. The letters support in many places what one might have conjectured about Thomas in the circumstances of that time: that as a kind of defence against the horror of the facts, while at the same time feeling the necessity for participating, he would not allow his full consciousness of things to emerge. He seems, for instance, to be admitting to a certain suspension of feeling and thought when in a letter to J. W. Haines, who had told him of the felling of some beautiful trees they had known, he writes:

> I don't think I shall regret the trees cut down till after it is all over, if I regret anything then.

And the self-explanation and self-analysis of the following passage from a letter to Helen gives a strong impression of his sense of the unreality of his present life:

> But I, you see, must not feel anything. I am just, as it were, tunnelling underground and something sensible in my subconscious directs me not to think of the sun, at the end of the tunnel there is the sun. Honestly, this is not the result of thinking; it is just an explanation of my state of mind which is really so entirely preoccupied with getting through the tunnel that you might say I had forgotten there was a sun at either end, before or after this business. This will perhaps induce you to call me inhuman like the newspapers, just because for a time I have had my ears stopped—mind you, I have not done it myself—to all but distant echoes of home and friends and England.

A good deal could be said about the state of mind and feeling manifested there: the knowledge of the limitedness of his life, the concentration and the willing that are necessary to live that life, the introspection, the courage, the clear-sightedness, the defensive caution, the perplexity, the apprehension. In the present context the point to be stressed is the suspension of his 'real' life, or, more accurately, the partial suspension, for he is still very much himself in the way he approaches his self-explanation, in his anxiety to understand and to justify himself, and in his desire that Helen should share his understanding.

I should say that what 'happiness' Thomas had at this time sprang in the main from his love of Helen and the children, from his contacts with nature either present or remembered, and from the knowledge that he was writing poetry that was good. That was a great thing for him, to be confident and pleased with what he was writing. I have dealt at some length on how I see Thomas and the war because when the soldier-poet aspect has been made much

of, when he has been used, naïvely or insidiously, as a
pawn for 'this England', not only is he being misunder-
stood or misrepresented as a man, but his poetry and what
he is really doing for England in and by his poetry are
being seen awry or not even seen at all.

In Thomas's disposition two of the traits that consistently helped to form a kind of positive or beneficent
force as against the negativeness of the self-distrust, the
isolation, the reticence—traits closely connected with each
other in that they stemmed from a common root of feeling—were a sense of the commonwealth of creatures and
things 'that the sun shines on', and a joy in the sight and
the thought of their separate and unique flowering into
life. The common root is sympathy. With a kind of moral
sensitiveness as true and delicate as his senses, he was
regardful of all life as it expressed itself in individual
beings and things; he was concerned that nothing should
be trampled on, and neither the demands of everyday
living nor his vexations and troubles caused him to miss
seeing the flowering or the frustration of life. This truly
equalizing and democratic spirit was intensely personal
in him and was never taken into the abstractions of
sociology and politics, though he was, as a matter of fact,
vaguely 'liberal and progressive', in tendency at least. The
trait under discussion is not that which showed itself in
more or less biting references to the 'pheasant lords' and
such-like, though this, too, must not be forgotten in our
view and estimate of Thomas; there are many such
references in his writings, and there is in *The Icknield Way*
a savagely ironical passage about

> A History of England for Shoe-Blacks and Sons of
> Gentlemen: or, A Guide to Tuft-Hunting, Sycophancy,
> Boot-licking, and other Services to the Aristocracy and
> Plutocracy, and to Keeping in Your Place.

The spirit I wish to suggest is that which may show itself at any moment in touches like this: '. . . the beeches lining the Roman road, and sheltering a gypsy camp among harebells, sweet basil, and trefoil, which the grasshopper also loves'; and this: '. . . flint-diggers' pathways, old roads and hares' paths lead over the Downs'. The hares and the grasshoppers share the earth with the humans; they have their dwelling-places and their paths. Thomas is rarely sentimental about this: he doesn't 'plead' for the small, or the fragile, or the ignored, or the scorned; he *notices* them, and reminds us they exist. He doesn't theorize or make out of his feelings any philosophy of universal love; he mentions, as he goes his way, the milk-white harebell that he sees growing on the grim crags of the hills of Wales. He doesn't preach that mud and eagles are equal in the eyes of God; mud really is to him interesting and beautiful (and not only useful) as he lightly refers to it. I am not suggesting that this sort of sympathy is bound to result in significant writing, but it must be emphasized as an essential part of Thomas's character and disposition; it is not at all the small matter that it may appear to be as manifested in quoted brief details. Of sympathy in the more usual sense—pity for the down-and-outs, the thwarted, the poor, the suffering—there is, of course, abundant evidence both in his writings and in the testimony of those who knew him.

'Equalizing' and 'democratic' sound perhaps rather ponderous as applied to something that was spontaneous and an impulse and not a system of thought or opinions, and it may be appropriate to repeat, especially for those who tend to associate uniformity with democracy, that the quality I have suggested as being integral in Thomas's character is one that recognizes 'skeined stained veined variety' and that sees with joy the growing and flowering of individual things or a particular beauty that may accrue to things with the passage of time. He shows us how the ordinary can blossom, and it is a quiet *thankfulness* that we feel in him for the flowering and the beauty. He sees 'dark spurge leaves *crowned* [my italics] by pale green flowers'; Abercorran House in *The Happy-Go-Lucky Morgans* is '*honoured* by four martins' nests under the eaves'. He never fails to be tenderly observant of new and young life and of the freshness that old life can take on:

> The trees were very old; their leaves were fresh and wet as when beauty and joy shed a few tears. The soil was centuries deep in black beech mast; the herbage seemed to have been born from it in that very hour. The boulders had stood among the primroses so long that the thrushes had chiselled shallow cups in them as they fed there in the mornings; they were embossed with the most tender green and golden moss. (*The Heart of England*)

When one day he meets with an abundance of primroses, he immediately thinks of a child's pleasure:

> The primrose roots hard by me had each sufficient flowers to make a child's handful. (*In Pursuit of Spring*)

And on a rough night he does not forget the harmony, secure while frail, of a dead flower and a butterfly:

> The rain will not come; the plunging wind in the trees has a sound of waterfalls all night, yet cannot trouble the sleep of the orange-tip butterfly on the leopard's-bane's dead flower. (*The South Country*)

It is not beyond imagining that a psychologist, concentrating on the 'cloud', might explain Thomas in terms of father-hate, or masochism through guilt, or the death-wish, or whatever else ministers to the desire for a neat and final understanding. Such an explanation, apart from the general unwisdom of attaching simplifying type-labels, would miss the man entirely. It is true that his finest expression of himself in words, namely his poetry, is 'about' his unhappiness; but it is also true that it is a poetry that makes for life. By the side of the character and mind that it reveals, most of his contemporaries in verse appear thin or trifling.

CHAPTER SIX

The Poetry

IT was through the encouragement and urging of Robert Frost that Thomas began writing the poetry that is his unique contribution to literature. The American poet, seeking in England the recognition he could not get in his own country, had become acquainted with the small group who had a cottage or two and a kind of headquarters in Gloucestershire (among them were Thomas himself, Rupert Brooke, Wilfrid Gibson, Lascelles Abercrombie, John Drinkwater), and sensing Thomas's potentialities Frost 'referred him to paragraphs in his book *In Pursuit of Spring* and told him to write it in verse form in exactly the same cadence' (Eckert). Thomas did not, of course, do exactly that, but the advice did have the effect of making him start. Later he wrote to Hudson: 'I had done no verses before, and did not expect to, and merely became nervous when I thought of beginning. But when it came to beginning I slipped into it naturally, whatever the results.' He spoke in a letter to John Freeman of his 'delight in the new freedom', and hoped that he wasn't 'too ready to accept intimations merely'.

Speculation as to why Thomas came so late to writing poetry is perhaps no more profitable than speculation as to what he might have gone on to write if war had not ended his life. Yet we have to wonder, if only in passing, why a man with such a care for literature, and having the temperament he had, should not have tried his hand until he was thirty-six years old. Perhaps the central reason lies precisely there: the whole character and temperament included what we call the 'poetic sensibility', but included also the reticence and the self-distrust. He was as little the fool that rushes in as a man can be, and his profound regard for the poet's place and function must have added weight to his innate cautiousness. That he had at least given thought to the possibility is clear from his words to Hudson quoted above: he 'did not expect to', and we note the characteristic restrained tone. He had a wholly serious view of the poet's calling, but his inspiration did not lie in any fervid thoughts of poets as 'the unacknowledged legislators of the world'. Possibly a contributory factor to the delay was a doubt induced by the amount of bad verse that came to his notice as a reviewer; he was the sort of man who would want to be sure that he was not encumbering the world with bad verse of his own. And as a further cause there was the fact that the living he had just managed to make over so many years came from his prose books: poetry could not have provided for Helen and the children. But clearly this last suggestion would be relevant only in the case of poetry for publication. It need not have held him back from writing it, and I am not aware that he ever complained of lack of time for writing poetry. Nevertheless, the time factor may have had something to do with it. If we combine it and its corollary, the arduousness and toil that much of the prose writing entailed, with the temperament as discussed above, we come perhaps as near as may be to the answer to a question which probably suggests itself at one time or another to all who are interested in Edward Thomas.

Little need be added here to what has been said in Chapter I about the fortunes of the poems as they were submitted, under the name of Edward Eastaway, to the various possible editors. It is a story of rejection all the way. Some of his acquaintances liked or made a show of liking them; Thomas was right in suspecting some of them of insincerity. Hudson and Harold Monro seem to have failed entirely to perceive the quality of the new writing that was being offered to them. Edward Garnett was enthusiastic about some of the poems, but the reservations he made about others were sometimes the effect of impercipience. Nevertheless, Garnett did try hard to get certain of the poems accepted; in 1917 he sent two, for instance, to *The Nation*, whose editor was H. W. Massingham, but they were not wanted.

Thomas knew too much about writers' lives to be unduly upset by his failure to secure publication. But behind the words of a letter that he sent to Monro with some of his poems, we feel among other things a certain anxiety and a touch of impatience, an anxiety, despite what he says about wanting his poems to be only liked, that they should be understood also:

> Let me know if any do [i.e. please him], but if any don't please don't tell me what you *think* of them,—for this reason, that I do not care a button what anybody thinks of them but I am at the same time excessively thin-skinned. I should have said I don't want to know what anyone thinks of them, whether favourable or not. But I am anxious to know if anyone really *likes* them or some or one of them.

The state of balance that must be held in the case of a man who is thin-skinned and at the same time doesn't care a button is a delicate one, and it is clear that Thomas felt something of the inward struggle and the tension or weariness that the need to explain involves; the new artist has to have much patience. But it is no less clear that Thomas was quite determined to go the way he thought best and right. He was always glad to listen to Garnett, and told him that he should certainly do his best against 'dimness and lack of concreteness', as he hated these things too much in others to tolerate them in himself; but he also told him that though his, Garnett's, preferences among his poems might help him to see where his mistakes lay he should risk some of them again, 'for example, what you find petty in incident'. There is still a caution in these letters about the poetry, and occasionally an undue deference caused by his innate self-distrust, but the self-criticism is now less simply dissatisfied in tone than it tended to be formerly, and there are unmistakable notes of a new assurance:

> I don't think I could alter *Tears* to make it marketable. I feel that the correction you want made is only essential if the whole point is in the British Grenadiers, as might be expected in these times. I can't be sure about the jog-trot. Perhaps you are right in finding it at the end of 'November', where it gets a shade sententious and perhaps echoes the end of the 'Sensitive Plant' in rhythm.

And again, writing to Garnett about *Lob*:

> I am doubtful about the chiselling you advise. It would be the easiest thing in the world to clean it all up and trim it and have every line straightforward in sound and sense, but it would not really improve it.

Thomas persisted, as Hopkins had persisted, in the defence of what he knew was right for himself. There is, in fact, occasionally an interesting specific parallel between statements and suggestions in the letters of the two poets. Here, for instance, is an excerpt from a letter of Hopkins to Bridges:

> Indeed, when, on somebody returning me the *Eurydice*, I opened and read some lines, as one commonly reads

whether prose or verse, with the eyes, so to say, only, it struck me aghast with a kind of raw nakedness and unmitigated violence I was unprepared for: but take breath and read it with the ears, as I always wish to be read, and my verse becomes all right.

And here is Thomas, still writing about *Lob*:

> I think you read too much with the eye perhaps. If you *say* a couplet like
>> If they had reaped their dandelions and sold
>> Them fairly, they could have afforded gold,
>
> I believe it is no longer awkward.

It was the effect of the speaking voice that Thomas most liked in Frost's poetry. But he did not himself set up simplicity and familiarity of diction and tone as an absolute. Defending Frost against criticisms by T. Sturge Moore, he points out in a letter to Bottomley that Frost doesn't want poetry to be merely colloquial:

> All he insists on is what he believes he finds in all poets —absolute fidelity to the postures which the voice assumes in the most expressive intimate speech. So long as these tones and postures are there he has not the least objection to any vocabulary whatever or any inversion or variation from the customary grammatical forms of talk. In fact I think he would agree that if these tones and postures survive in a complicated and learned or subtle vocabulary and structure the result is likely to be better than if they survive in the easiest form, that is, in the very words and structures of common speech. . . .

Thomas wanted to get the expressive tones of the speaking voice into his own poetry; he told Eleanor Farjeon that if he was consciously doing anything it was 'trying to get rid of the last rags of rhetoric and formality which left my prose so often with a dead rhythm'. And the tones, the living rhythm, will, of course, spring from feeling: 'Con-centration, intensity of mood, is the one necessary condi-tion in the poet and in the poem', he says in *Maeterlinck*. And in 1915 he wrote to John Freeman:

> What I have done so far have been like quintessences of the best parts of my prose books—not much sharper or more intense, but I hope a little.

In the light of this remark about 'quintessences' it will be interesting to glance at a few of the verbal and other correspondences between the prose and the poetry. Later we shall see more fully what rich development in Thomas the new sharpness and intensity were both sign and record of.

The correspondences are very numerous. It is clear that for Thomas the poetic creative process involved among other things the recollection of incidents and scenes which had already been written about in the prose, and that perceptions and phrases came back to him to be in-corporated in the poetry with a new significance. The details of an October description in *Wales* appear in the poem *October*, and become there a part of the presentment and description of a mood and not only of a scene. The jackdaw in *The South Country*—

> Another day, a wide and windy day, is the jackdaw's, and he goes straight and swift and high like a joyous rider crying aloud on an endless savannah

—conveys a sense of swift joyous life and 'endless' is here positive and exultant; in the poem *Ambition* (to be ex-amined later), the bird still goes 'straight and high', but it has taken on a richer symbolic value in its being an integral part of a larger and more complex experience. The thrush that sings 'over and over again', the feeling of being 'an old inhabitant of the earth', the shepherd's

'Ho! Ho!' to his sheep, the 'Indian complexion' of Jack Horseman, the man or woman who has 'no tears left', the natural creatures that can 'do no wrong', are but a few of the scores of phrases or thoughts that reappear in the poetry. And occasionally a prose cadence unites with the diction to remind us of something in the poetry: 'The sun in the sky was the one thing that moved' (*Light and Twilight*) will recall for many readers one of the key lines of *Wind and Mist*: 'The flint was the one crop that never failed.'

We shall find that the new economy and sharpness in the poetry, and even the more perfectly suggested beauty and particular quality of the sensuous perceptions, are not matters only of a greater skill in words but that they are an indication of development in its widest sense, growth of sensibility and character. It would be easy to demonstrate how the poetry's presentation of the 'joy-sadness' mood is more subtle and more mature than the explicit accounts in the prose, however thoughtful these may be, of what is ostensibly the same condition; how the feelings which in the prose gave rise to statements like 'Light and warmth and fellowship are good', which spoke of, say, 'living on the edge of eternity', or of the 'mysterious aloofness' of trees, receive a finer definition in the poetry and come home to us with the living and vivid expression of art; how the early 'puissant' silences and the sometimes 'literary' rain (real and strong though the original sensations and apprehensions were), gave way to grasped actualities which at the same time had a profounder spiritual meaning for the poet; and how in general the greater significance is conveyed with a proportionately lighter touch.

Of the hundred and forty or so poems, between eighty and ninety are what we may for the moment call nature poems; there are some eighteen love poems, six or seven war poems, a dozen poems of the 'direct statement' kind, using more or less explicit statements to convey his condition and his thought, and about twenty 'miscellaneous' poems. Such a classification is, of course, approximate; moreover, it is offered as having no more than a certain information value. It must also be added immediately that 'nature poems' is only a heading for convenience; they are 'human nature' poems too, and the central interest is not in their nature content, rich and unique as that is.

Thomas had, of course, the 'eye' that is commonly (and too often glibly) attributed to nature poets. Many of his poems have their origin—or their apparent, their immediate origin—in something seen with the kind of particularity that is a warrant of love:

> They have taken the gable from the roof of clay
> On the long swede pile. They have let in the sun
> To the white and gold and purple of curled fronds
> Unsunned. It is a sight more tender-gorgeous
> At the wood-corner where Winter moans and drips
> Than when . . .   (*Swedes*)

Pictorial details and images abound:

> The swift with wings and tail as sharp and narrow
> As if the bow had flown off with the arrow.
>   (*Haymaking*)

> The leaflets out of the ash-tree shed
> Are thinly spread
> In the road, like little black fish, inlaid,
> As if they played.   (*After Rain*)

> The path, winding like silver, trickles on,
> Bordered and even invaded by thinnest moss
> That tries to cover roots and crumbling chalk
> With gold, olive, and emerald, but in vain.
> The children wear it.   (*The Path*)

Thomas's 'clear eye' was a source of joy to him. But the eye's delight in colour, shape, motion, is by itself not likely to make poetry of any very great substantiality, and with Thomas, seeing and (we may add) listening and hearing were usually only the beginning—again, we must use the word diffidently—of the deeper and subtler experience presented in the poetry. Middleton Murry has put it this way:'. . . But these objects of vision were but the occasion of the more profound discoveries within the region of his own soul.' Another way of putting it would be: the particular quality of his mind, that quality and character that his mind had grown and gathered through the years of living, often found its characteristic expression by way of a moment's seeing or hearing. (Mr Murry's 1919 article on Thomas's poetry—it was a review of the *Last Poems*—is reprinted in *Aspects of Literature*. The article shows signs of the stress of the times and of the author: Thomas is seen as a kind of refuge, because he speaks a truth or truths, in a world of horror, and at times the tone of eloquent ecstasy with which Mr Murry welcomes him seems to tell us more about the critic than about the poet. He seems to see Thomas as the one preserver of the 'subtler faiths' which 'so easily might have fled through our harsh fingers'. Nevertheless, he points with a fine insight to some of the essentials, and with an emphasis which, the directing intelligence in those places being what it was, ought to have had more effect than it seemingly did have. He indicates the peculiar elusiveness of the poet's spirit, his knowledge of certain deep and unfamiliar truths, the nature of his search for the beautiful; he states his belief that Thomas has 'many of the qualities of a great poet'. And despite the recurring floweriness and portentousness, the tone and manner sometimes unduly revelatory of the critic's own state of anxiety and of his own philosophy, despite the curious last sentence which seems to nullify much of what he has previously said ['But if his compositions do not, his themes will never fail—of so much we are sure—to awaken unsuspected echoes even in unsuspecting minds'], Mr Murry's article remains one of the few that admirers of Thomas will want to go back to.)

When on a fresh spring-like July evening a 'stranger' said to Thomas, then a young man, 'The lattermath will be a fine one', the words were taken simultaneously in their literal and metaphorical senses, and the meadows among which they were spoken were also, to the poet, the 'meadows of the future', which he, 'flushed with desire', seemed already to possess; so that when he recalls the stranger's words on a similar July evening twenty years later, they come back to him as an 'unaccomplished prophecy'. What had taken place on the plane of every-day intercourse was imbued with a quality that gave it a deeper, an inner meaning. The instance cited is, of course, a simple enough one, being dependent upon spontaneously applying 'lattermath' to fields and to life. 'Spontaneously' is the important word here: there is no self-consciousness, no sense of strain or manufacture in Thomas's 'double' perceptiveness and his expression of it. It is not insisted upon, it doesn't advertise itself. We have to be on the alert even with the less complex poems: in *Early One Morning in May I Set Out*, for instance, with its apparent careless light-heartedness, we are likely at first to miss the full significance of the refrain:

> I'm bound away for ever,
> Away somewhere, away for ever.

And in *The Sign-Post*, after he has described the late-autumn scene 'at the hilltop by the finger-post', and has said:

> I read the sign. Which way shall I go?

THE POETRY

we are led with the lightest possible touch, and with no
semblance of forcing, into poetry which is 'about' freedom
of choice. He reads what it says on the finger-post; and
he reads the 'sign', the reminder that is given by the scene
of summer's passing; and he wonders which way he will
go.

Here now is a complete short poem, *The Hollow Wood*:

> Out in the sun the goldfinch flits
> Along the thistle-tops, flits and twits
> Above the hollow wood
> Where birds swim like fish—
> Fish that laugh and shriek—
> To and fro, far below
> In the pale hollow wood.
>
> Lichen, ivy, and moss
> Keep evergreen the trees
> That stand half-flayed and dying,
> And the dead trees on their knees
> In dog's-mercury and moss:
> And the bright twit of the goldfinch drops
> Down there as he flits on thistle-tops.

Thomas doesn't often cross his t's and dot his i's as he does
here; but even so the onomatopœia is not of the same
order as 'The long wash of Australasian seas': it is not the
all-in-all, and it could readily be shown that the movements and sounds, the stillness, the hollowness, suggested
by the sound-qualities and the tempo of the words belong
integrally to the whole thought-and-feeling experience of
the poem. But what it is wished most to emphasize here is
what F. R. Leavis has called attention to when writing of
Thomas in *New Bearings in English Poetry*: 'the inner life
which the sensory impressions are notation for.' (Dr
Leavis's note seems to me to be *the* one to which everyone
interested in Thomas can be recommended, the more so

for its context in the account of the general situation in poetry during the first quarter or so of the century. The present book is deeply indebted to it.) Out of something seemingly slight, something from which a lesser poet might perhaps have made a pleasant poem of externals, Thomas's way of experiencing makes something comparatively profound. We find that 'descriptive' would be an inadequate epithet for the poem. We notice, for instance, a co-presence of elements which, if they were not here given us bound together in a natural and harmonious scene, we should probably feel to be disparate: there is some startling 'seeing', and there is an implicit contrast between what we may (rather heavy-handedly) call life-and-death symbols. And yet it is all 'life': a curiously moving effect comes from the sense the poem gives of a unity among things which could be said to be at war with one another. The light flitting of the bird, a (brilliant) goldfinch, on the light thistle-tops, and the 'bright twit' of its song in the sun, exist alongside the 'pale hollow wood' where trees are dead and dying. 'Lichen, ivy, and moss' are alive and are beautiful, but they are all parasites too, and so 'Keep evergreen' is in part, but *only* in part, ironic; dog's-mercury is a plant with poisonous properties. The birds in the wood below are as if in another element than their own; they are seen, in a moment of seeing that is vividly surprising and true, as 'fish that laugh and shriek'. We are a long way from St Francis's 'little sisters, the birds'. The drop of bird-song falls into a kind of unearthly underwater world and is lost there. And though the last image is of the quick-moving bird, what the title stands for—*The Hollow Wood*—always makes itself felt in the poetry. Any philosophy or metaphysical idea we may care to abstract is not, of course, necessarily valuable in its own right. It is the poetry that holds the value, presenting a way of seeing and feeling that has depth and innerness while still remaining fresh and physical.

Thomas does make overt statements, he ponders, he expresses 'thoughts'. Not all his poems are so entirely metaphorical and so little expository as *The Hollow Wood*. And when his thinking and his comments come in naturally with his described scenes and situations, as they almost always beautifully do, there are gains in fullness and variety. Such gains can be seen in a poem like *Old Man*, but for the moment our main concern is still with the way in which the details of the incident and scene are developed to convey the inner world of the poet's feeling and thought:

> Old Man, or Lad's-Love,—in the name there's nothing
> To one that knows not Lad's-Love, or Old Man,
> The hoar-green feathery herb, almost a tree,
> Growing with rosemary and lavender.
> Even to one that knows it well, the names
> Half decorate, half perplex, the thing it is:
> At least, what that is clings not to the names
> In spite of time. And yet I like the names.
>
> The herb itself I like not, but for certain
> I love it, as some day the child will love it
> Who plucks a feather from the door-side bush
> Whenever she goes in or out of the house.
> Often she waits there, snipping the tips and shrivelling
> The shreds at last on to the path, perhaps
> Thinking, perhaps of nothing, till she sniffs
> Her fingers and runs off. The bush is still
> But half as tall as she, though it is as old;
> So well she clips it. Not a word she says;
> And I can only wonder how much hereafter
> She will remember, with that bitter scent,
> Of garden rows, and ancient damson trees
> Topping a hedge, a bent path to a door,

A low thick bush beside the door, and me
Forbidding her to pick.

                    As for myself,
Where first I met the bitter scent is lost.
I, too, often shrivel the grey shreds,
Sniff them and think and sniff again and try
Once more to think what it is I am remembering,
Always in vain. I cannot like the scent,
Yet I would rather give up others more sweet,
With no meaning, than this bitter one.

I have mislaid the key. I sniff the spray
And think of nothing; I see and I hear nothing;
Yet seem too, to be listening, lying in wait
For what I should, yet never can, remember:
No garden appears, no path, no hoar-green bush
Of Lad's-Love, or Old Man, no child beside,
Neither father nor mother, nor any playmate;
Only an avenue, dark, nameless, without end.

For our immediate purpose we can note, in this beautiful poem, the unobtrusive way he puts the 'garden rows, and ancient damson trees', with their plenty and sweetness, next to 'that bitter scent'; then there is the implicit significant contrast of the seen and named with the nameless—the discussed names of the plant, the familiar and man-made 'bent path to a door', and the 'avenue, dark, nameless, without end': two ways of perceiving, the social-everyday and the individual-profound, are simultaneously present. The passage of time is subtly and variously suggested: there are the child and the grown-up, the ancient trees, the two names of the plant, Lad's-Love and Old Man, the description of the plant as 'the hoar-green feathery herb, almost a tree'; 'shrivelling the grey shreds' is similarly evocative. There are characteristic undertones: the bitter scent, for instance—'Where first I met the bitter scent is lost'—is not the smell of the plant only, and this scent (giving a depth to the understanding, giving more experience) is preferred to 'others more sweet, With no meaning'.

Old Man has the quiet tone, the expressive movement, and the unassuming diction that combine to make the kind of art by which Thomas recorded his experience. It is ultimately in the art, not in the eye, nor in the deeper vision, nor in the sympathies, but in the art which includes all those and which 'bids us touch and taste and hear and see the world' (W. B. Yeats), that we discern and fully feel Thomas's quality. We may look profitably at *March* as richly showing that quality:

> Now I know that Spring will come again,
> Perhaps to-morrow: however late I've patience
> After this night following on such a day.
>
> While still my temples ached from the cold burning
> Of hail and wind, and still the primroses
> Torn by the hail were covered up in it,
> The sun filled earth and heaven with a great light
> And a tenderness, almost warmth, where the hail dripped,
> As if the mighty sun wept tears of joy.
> But 'twas too late for warmth. The sunset piled
> Mountains on mountains of snow and ice in the west:
> Somewhere among their folds the wind was lost,
> And yet 'twas cold, and though I knew that Spring
> Would come again, I knew it had not come,
> That it was lost too in those mountains chill.
>
> What did the thrushes know? Rain, snow, sleet, hail,
> Had kept them quiet as the primroses.
> They had but an hour to sing. On boughs they sang,
> On gates, on ground; they sang while they changed perches
> And while they fought, if they remembered to fight:
> So earnest were they to pack into that hour
> Their unwilling hoard of song before the moon
> Grew brighter than the clouds. Then 'twas no time

For singing merely. So they could keep off silence
And night, they cared not what they sang or screamed;
Whether 'twas hoarse or sweet or fierce or soft;
And to me all was sweet: they could do no wrong.
Something they knew—I also, while they sang
And after. Not till night had half its stars
And never a cloud, was I aware of silence
Stained with all that hour's songs, a silence
Saying that Spring returns, perhaps to-morrow.

Here we are brought, through the perfection of the technique, extraordinarily close to the sensations and feelings of the poet; and yet we are aware all the time that the poem comes to more than a communication of the sensations and feelings caused by outward happenings. The physical events and effects of the day have been felt keenly and delicately, and at the same time the discomfort of the cold, the joy in the thrushes, the awareness of silence (and so on) have a more than physical, more than sensuous significance, and the spring is happiness without ceasing to be spring. The poem has character and mind in it and not simply fine sensuous perceptiveness. There are the characteristic qualifications: 'perhaps to-morrow', 'almost warmth', 'however late'; and we feel the full force of those 'mountains chill' (the adjective being finely placed at the end of the line, and deriving a further emphasis from its association, through rhyme, with 'still', which has itself occurred twice). But with all the seeming caution and reserve, and though the temples ached with cold, his senses and heart and mind are open to, sharply alive to, the world about him: the sense of bounty is stronger than the feeling of discomfort and deprivation. The gratitude is for an outpouring that comes from an '*unwilling* hoard'—life pouring itself out without calculation and self-regard—and then beautifully for the silence that follows. The uncertainty, the hope or the doubt expressed in the last words, 'perhaps to-morrow', doesn't impair his perceiving sensitively and clearly here and now. The attitude towards life that the poem conveys is 'un-Georgian' in its not being conditioned by any preconceptions as to what beauty in nature is or by any tendency to moralize; the belief or the knowledge that the poem expresses is about as far away as can be from the conventional general-cheerful kind of hope which comes of a simplification of experience. Thomas's response is his own; it is fresh and it is subtle. Note, for instance, in this poem, the delicate manner in which he indicates that the distress of the cold and storm is not his alone: the reference to the torn primroses is of the same length and has almost the same weight and rhythm as the line and a half about his aching temples; and when he asks in the first half of a line, 'What did the thrushes know?', the second half of the line supplies at least an important part of the answer, although it is syntactically connected with the following line. That same question, 'What did the thrushes know?' balances the 'Now I know' of the opening, and suggests a different way of knowing: and towards the end of the poem the thought of the difference is given more explicitly, the significantly-placed 'And after' suggesting the faculty which he has and they have not. Note how the word 'tenderness' is linked by unobtrusive alliteration with 'torn'. This tenderness, a tenderness of colour or hue as well as of feeling, comes from the sun but would not be there but for the icy hail, nor is it to last: the full, thankful line, 'As if the mighty sun wept tears of joy', is immediately followed by the quietly definite 'But 'twas too late for warmth'. Later in the poem, we feel the silence not only as something enjoyed and as perhaps heralding a near spring but also as the silence which always comes back and which exists at the back of every sound; we note too that for the poet the silence was *stained*, equivocally but not deprecatingly—stain may beautify or mar, or beautify while it mars—'Stained with all that hour's songs'. The dying-off of the medley of sounds, which had persisted in his consciousness for some time after they had actually ceased, and his becoming aware of silence, are present and realized in the poetry, felt in the varying weight and emphasis and tempo of the words, and throughout the poem the changes in the force and direction of his feelings and thoughts—feeling and thought seeming one and the same thing and in perfect correspondence with the sensuous experience as it develops—are a matter of subtle living growth: we watch and listen to the whole experience as it comes into life in the words. The movement of the words, which is, of course, integral to this effect of naturalness and inevitability, is alive with the variations of speech-movement. We seem to be listening to a poet *speaking* easily and fluently but with beautiful precision, revealing something of his inner life, his spirit, by an extraordinarily sensitive account of an experience of the outer world.

To attribute precision of feeling to a poet who never finally satisfied himself as to the cause of his most characteristic mood or state of mind will not appear out of place so long as we do not confuse precise feeling with complete self-knowledge. Within the situation and mood of his poems Thomas defines his feelings scrupulously. It may be true that something held him back from the fullest kind of self-exposure, that he did not put as many situations, as many of his feelings, as much of his life, into his poetry as he himself might have wished to do. But *within* his range the truth and the sensitiveness are unquestionable: outer scene and the response to it, or, conversely, state of mind and the sensuous experience which in some way reflects it and gives it form, are rendered with the kind of delicate statement of emotion that we associate with music.

If we say that there is no *Ode to Autumn* among Thomas's poems, it is to suggest an effect for his poetry of that characteristic in him which in the discussion of *March* was rather tentatively called 'caution' or 'reserve'. Whether or not we wish to find a philosophy in Keats's great poem, we can say that it does represent a fulfilled state of being: the poet is rich with a satisfaction which is not impaired by the hints he gives of coming winter. There is no fulfilment of that kind in Thomas's poetry. An almost ever-present sense of an elusive element in consciousness, a habit of recalling and trying to recall, of looking forward and wondering, must tend to prevent the achievement of a full richness and intensity. No one could be more aware of this than Thomas himself was; and, in fact, this very awareness is an explicit theme in the poetry. In *The Glory*, a poem that perfectly integrates description of the morning's beauty with pondering on the nature of beauty and of happiness, he writes:

> The glory invites me, yet it leaves me scorning
> All I can ever do, all I can be,
> Beside the lovely of motion, shape, and hue,
> The happiness I fancy fit to dwell
> In beauty's presence.

And the poem ends with this:

> And shall I ask at the day's end once more
> What beauty is, and what I can have meant
> By happiness? And shall I let all go,
> Glad, weary, or both? Or shall I perhaps know
> That I was happy oft and oft before,
> Awhile forgetting how I am fast pent,
> How dreary-swift, with naught to travel to,
> Is Time? I cannot bite the day to the core.

Such a consciousness of time as that last line or two reveal would by itself have made it impossible for Thomas to 'bite the day to the core'. Greatly as he 'loved' the months and the seasons, it was never any simple feeling of strength or fitness or rejoicing that the thought of their eternal recurrence brought to him. He never expressed a conclusion like that which Hawthorne comes to in the second half of the passage quoted below, when writing of the beginnings of spring (in an essay called 'Buds and Bird Voices'):

> Some tracts in a happy exposure, as, for instance, yonder south-western slope of an orchard, in front of that old red farm house beyond the river, such patches of land already wear a beautiful and tender green, to which no future luxuriance can add a charm. It looks unreal; a prophecy, a hope, a transitory effect of some peculiar light, which will vanish with the slightest motion of the eye. But beauty is never a delusion; not these verdant tracts, but the dark and barren landscape all around them, is a shadow and a dream. Each moment wins some portion of the earth from death to life; a sudden gleam of verdure brightens along the sunny slope of a bank which an instant ago was brown and bare. You look again, and behold an apparition of green grass!

Thomas was never moved to express a confidence like this as to what is real and what is delusion. Nor, on the other hand, was he ever like Hardy in giving, through the Egdon Heath description for instance, a solid anti-Hawthornian view. Thomas has no solid views. In this matter of change and time he is perhaps more likely to remind us of an aspect of Mr Eliot's poetry than of either of the nine-teenth-century writers as referred to above:

> There is no end, but addition: the trailing
> Consequence of further days and hours.

But Thomas's weariness is not so dismal as Mr Eliot's sometimes is. (Hawthorne's formulated optimistic conclusion, it may be pointed out, is a conscious viewpoint, and is, of course, a much more simple affair than the attitudes conveyed in his writings as a whole. And, as a matter of fact, there are some close and fundamental similarities between Hawthorne and Thomas in the way they perceive nature. This is not the place to develop such a proposition, but I believe that anyone who knows something of Thomas's attitudes and feelings would be struck by the frequency he would be reminded of them in a reading of Hawthorne. I say this after a recent reading of *Mosses from an Old Manse*, where time and again emphasis is put on things which recall Thomas both in a general way and in actual verbal details.)

It is interesting to note that although he cannot 'bite the day to the core', the language and the image that he uses to tell us this have a strength and a sharpness which show at least that he knows fully what 'biting' means and involves. Moreover, the poetry abounds with concreteness, with tangible life. His capacity for an extraordinarily keen enjoyment of the things of the world around him, the sense almost of happiness in being simply a man 'Standing upright out in the air' (even though this thought came probably from the thought of lying in the grave) was never effaced by the consciousness of being also a 'ghost' who watches the peewits and 'wonders why So merrily they cry and fly'. Reading Thomas, we are in fact often reminded of Keats's delight in natural beautiful things; and though Thomas's enjoyment was not embodied in poetry as magnificently rich and strong as Keats's best, I would say that it came from a contact with the natural world even more close and delicate.

This closeness and delicacy, which is so much more than

a matter of visual Tennysonian accuracy, is present with an astonishing consistency in Thomas's poetry. In *Birds' Nests*, where he is glad at finding in winter the nests he had missed in spring, he writes of a certain deep-hid nest:

> Once a dormouse dined there on hazel-nuts,
> And grass and goose-grass seeds found soil and grew.

The tenderness of his interest is felt particularly, I think, in 'found soil', this kindly soil that had been mud binding the grasses and straws of the nest when it was built in spring, and nourishing new grass and goose-grass after nesting operations had finished and the nest been long deserted; one thinks of the minute seeds chancing on that bit of soil. *It Rains* ends thus:

> When I turn away, on its fine stalk
> Twilight has fined to naught, the parsley flower
> Figures, suspended still and ghostly white,
> The past hovering as it revisits the light.

And the following lines are from *There's Nothing like the Sun*:

> The south wall warms me; November has begun,
> Yet never shone the sun as fair as now
> While the sweet last-left damsons from the bough
> With spangles of the morning's storm drop down
> Because the starling shakes it, whistling what
> Once swallows sang.

Passages like these have a finely sensuous quality in their detail, detail which is offered so unassumingly. Many of the details have an inner significance too, and his way of conveying significances is likewise quiet and the reverse of rhetorical. In the first of these three passages the things seen suggest the perpetual mingling of the ripened and finished with the growing and new, death and birth in nature. Then 'ghostly white' will be seen to be no pictorial or emotive cliché but to have (in addition to its sensuous value) its precise meaning in relation to the experience of recalling round which the poem is built. And the last words of the third passage, 'whistling what Once swallows sang', do more than tell us that one of the starling's voices is an imitation of the swallow's; for besides holding a tinge of regret in their hinting at the passing of summer—summer embodied in the swallow's song—they also accept the starling's 'whistling' as a beautiful manifestation of life, as an expression, a *voice* of life; the whistling is *with* all the colour and sweetness. Similarly, the damsons, though they are the 'last-left' and though their hold is so frail—they fall from the same shaking as makes the raindrops fall—are 'sweet', and bright with the 'spangles of the morning's storm'.

Sensuous details in a Thomas poem are rarely piled up for their own sake; there is nothing in his poetry like the loose and unorganized abundance of, say, *Endymion*. He gathers his details together purposefully, and the sensuous perceptions are a meaningful, integral element in the whole *vision*, the whole experience that a poem is. *Ambition* will help to show how details accumulate to form an experience, an experience in which the poet's reflections come in easily and, as it were, inevitably blended with the sensuous perceptiveness:

Unless it was that day I never knew
Ambition. After a night of frost, before
The March sun brightened and the South-west blew,
Jackdaws began to shout and float and soar
Already, and one was racing straight and high
Alone, shouting like a black warrior
Challenges and menaces to the wide sky.
With loud long laughter then a woodpecker
Ridiculed the sadness of the owl's last cry.

And through the valley where all the folk astir
Made only plumes of pearly smoke to tower
Over dark trees and white meadows happier
Than was Elysium in that happy hour,
A train that roared along raised after it
And carried with it a motionless white bower
Of purest cloud, from end to end close-knit,
So fair it touched the roar with silence. Time
Was powerless while that lasted. I could sit
And think I had made the loveliness of prime,
Breathed its life into it and were its lord,
And no mind lived save this 'twixt clouds and rime.
Omnipotent I was, nor even deplored
That I did nothing. But the end fell like a bell:
The bower was scattered; far off the train roared.
But if this was ambition I cannot tell.
What 'twas ambition for I know not well.

The subtlety of the experience presented here doesn't
depend unduly on the elusiveness of the nature of the
ambition that the poet felt. It springs mainly from the
extraordinary interplay of images of energetic life with a
sense of silence, of sadness, of emptiness. The jackdaws are
full of boisterous life 'already', in the cold morning; but
the shouts of the bird detached from its companions,
although it races 'straight and high' (the truth of the
physical observation is beautifully in evidence), seem to
spring as much from defiance as from exultation, and the
'challenges and menaces to the wide sky', the sky which
doesn't hear and which remains for ever unmoved, are
felt to be futile even while they are vital and courageous;
the woodpecker laughs at the sad owl, but the ridicule is
rather too noisy to be wholly self-assured and seems moreover to have needed the encouragement of the 'black
warrior'; all the doings of the 'folk astir' make only
'plumes of pearly smoke', smoke that brings to the poet's

mind Elysium with its opposing yet linked associations of bliss and death; the roaring moving train carries with it a motionless bower of cloud, and of silence. *Ambition* is one of several poems (*Haymaking*, *The Green Roads*, *The Brook*, *Tears*, are others), which make it understandable that some critics have been tempted to be satisfied with calling Thomas a mystic:

> So fair it touched the roar with silence. Time
> Was powerless while that lasted.

But 'mystical' is too vague a term to be very useful; it suggests itself here, probably, not only because of the idea of timelessness but because we are made to share to some extent the poet's state, a state in which wondering and almost pondering seem to exist along with an absorption, an intense interest, in the present moment. But though he may seem to be strangely suspended between the clouds and the earth, the grasp of the actual makes us firmly discard 'mystical': with the obscure nature of the prompting mood goes an astonishing clarity of sensuous perceiving. And the actual is felt as both livingly beautiful and unsatisfying; the bower was scattered.

It is misleading to speak of this poet as 'utterly at home in the world of nature': the words are John Freeman's, and the view they state is that of many who have written about Thomas. Of course, he lived in the country when he was free to choose, and he knew the country and 'loved' it with a depth hardly surpassable; and his life in the country was crowded year after year with moments that had an extraordinary value for him. But those moments cannot be characterized as a simple resting in the beauty of nature. Sometimes we may care to say that he does rest so: there is a day when he 'thinks Only with scents', when

> a bonfire burns
> The dead, the waste, the dangerous,
> And all to sweetness turns.

> It is enough
> To smell, to crumble the dark earth;

another day when he lies in a boat and watches and listens through the hours of a July dawn, in a 'drowse of heat and solitude afloat':

> All that the ring-doves say, far leaves among,
> Brims my mind with content thus still to lie;

and the *thankfulness* is to be felt everywhere in the poetry:

> And what blue and what white is I never knew
> Before I saw this sky blessing the land.

But taking the poetry as a whole, I do not think it can usefully be said that Thomas was at home in nature, in the unqualified sense intended by some of his admirers, any more than Wordsworth was 'at home' in most of the vividly lived moments described in *The Prelude*. There were not perhaps for Thomas the 'severer interventions' that there were for Wordsworth, nor the claimed moral chastening, but there was something that nevertheless worked effectively against 'at-home-ness'; there is the element represented in these lines from the well-known *Out in the Dark*:

> And star and I and wind and deer,
> Are in the dark together,—near,
> Yet far,—and fear
> Drums on my ear
> In that sage company drear.

'The dark' is more than physical; and in general, to recall Dr Leavis's words, 'the intimations that come are not of immortality'. *Out in the Dark* is, of course, a poem of night-time, but in nearly all the poetry the awareness, felt and not only pondered, of an unknown element in life modifies the 'enjoyment' of the moment even while it subtilizes and enriches it. One would have thought that Thomas's numerous explicit references to his sense of something remote and hard to capture and yet very real to him, would in themselves have been enough to prevent a discerning reader from forming such a decided impression as Freeman's 'utterly at home' suggests. In gathering one or two of these references for quotation one becomes aware how perfectly they are part of a whole poem and how they lose by being extracted. Nevertheless, they do suggest something of that remoteness in consciousness. He is haunted by the memory of an old chalk-pit, silent, empty, still, which on the two or three occasions when he had seen it had curiously seemed to him to have been, just before his visit, 'full Of life of some kind, perhaps tragical':

> Again and again I see it, strangely dark,
> And vacant of a life but just withdrawn.
> (*The Chalk-Pit*)

He is moved by a certain valley-scene with its small river, its cattle and grass, its bare ash trees:

> I never expected anything
> Nor yet remembered: but some goal
> I touched then.
> (*I Never Saw that Land Before*)

He often introduces into his poetry the idea of touching a goal; and touching is not resting. I should say that if there was anything that Thomas at that time of his life can be said to have not touched but reached and rested in, it was the certainty of his knowledge that he was finding in poetry, despite the 'melancholy' that suffuses it, his finest mode of expression.

In discussing the 'melancholy' in the poetry—Thomas uses the word often but never simply as a description of the mood or state—we are concerned with it as it is part of the whole sensibility and not as having an autonomous psychological interest. The total consciousness out of which the poetry comes is far too complex to be even faintly indicated by the word 'melancholy', and the poetry is, in fact, an affirmation (not in the Browningesque manner) of life and living. It is remarkable that in a poetry that lacks the strength of tragedy—it is not impersonal enough to achieve that kind of strength—and which is so much concerned with 'unhappiness', there should be so much positive life. The poetry shows, as all art does, that it is what a man makes of his experience that matters most.

With this in mind, we may glance at some of the named sources of Thomas's unhappiness or dissatisfaction, sources given more or less explicit mention in the poetry: there are thoughts of death, his own death, and that of friends, of soldiers, of creatures; painful memories of past happiness; inability to foresee and control the future; fear of solitude, and of company; the fact of transience and change in men and men's lives, in things; failure to 'understand or alter or prevent'; inability to relive past happy hours, and at the same time inability to forget them; the harshness of the 'real' ('But flint and clay and childbirth were too real For this cloud-castle', he says, writing of a house on a hill that he had lived in); the difficulties attendant upon free choice, 'freedom to wish'; idealism disappointed; the remoteness and elusiveness of beauty, of happiness, of peace, as absolutes; imperfect health; the sadness of parting from friendly people; the 'dreary-swift' journeying of Time, 'with naught to travel to'. This catalogue of ideas and themes, taken by themselves, might well raise misgivings as to the poetry which should utilize them. But Thomas's poetry is as fresh as any in the language: he never uses an abstract concept or thought as a peg to hang a poem on, and it is, in fact, rare that any of those listed above is made the central interest in a poem by him. The total experience in which they find mention is very much more than a matter of regrets, longings, despairs. When we give our full attention to the experience that the poetry is, it becomes plain that Thomas's *malaise* is not to be accounted for simply by the pressure of such thoughts.

It would be obtuse to say that Thomas was immature because he could not exactly 'explain' his discontent. Maturity is not a fixed value, there is a greater and a less; and there is a sense in which we can call Donne mature, and Jane Austen, though neither of them is Shakespeare. We shall probably not care to go further than to suggest that there is something *relatively* immature in the way Thomas often refers to happiness and beauty as 'goals' that can conceivably be reached and retained, as if he hoped a golden land existed at the end of a journey. He was never, of course, a romantic yearner; he was never complacent, he was always questioning himself. But his frequent longing for a perfect 'home' seems to be an inevitable outcome of his failure to achieve the kind of integration that we associate with a great tragic poet, the adjustment that comes with passing through personal suffering to a more inclusive vision and view of life. It is only in so far as he did not present such a vision, with its corollary of a rich and varied objectivity, that we might say Thomas was immature.

In the lovely poem, *Beauty*, after saying that no man, woman, or child could please him now, and after comparing himself (with what delicate precision) to

> a river
> At fall of evening while it seems that never
> Has the sun lighted it or warmed it, while
> Cross breezes cut the surface to a file,

he looks through the window to a tree 'Down in the mist-
ing, dim-lit quiet vale', and 'like a dove That slants un-
swerving to its home and love', he finds beauty there:
'There I find my rest'. This brief summary gives an inadequate impression of the poem, and is intended only to
show that the impulse to escape to a blissful simplicity is
there. But we shall see that there is always something in
Thomas that prevents anything like a full surrender being
made. The 'easy hours' which were an essential part of
his life—

> And other men through other flowers
> In those fields under the same moon
> Go talking and have easy hours

—never involved a defection of intelligence; his senses and
his spirit were alert even while he refreshed himself with
such hours. He can, in *Haymaking*, compare the clouds in
the 'perfect blue' to the

> first gods before they made the world
> And misery, swimming the stormless sea
> In beauty and in divine gaiety,

and the tone has something of the longing that goes with
the dream of a golden land, and the thought of the 'divine
gaiety' of the gods seems to rise out of a dissatisfaction
with the moral-and-social restrictiveness of everyday
human life; but there is no 'immature' chafing or rebel-
lion, and there follows in the poem a finely detailed
description which reveals the poet not dreaming of an

easy Utopia, but firmly and sensitively and intelligently alive on the earth where he stands.

That Thomas felt the burden of mental consciousness to be heavy is unquestionable; his references to the simple spontaneity of non-human creatures are often of the idealizing, half-envious kind: in the thrushes' 'proverbs untranslateable', he hints, is something finer than human wisdom, and he is explicit at the end of *Sedge-Warblers*:

> This was the best of May—the small brown birds
> Wisely reiterating endlessly
> What no man learnt yet, in or out of school.

Thomas's response to wild creatures was deeply loving and exquisitely sensitive, but in the way he expressed the attractiveness and sometimes the mystery of their 'otherness' he was momentarily liable to betray some desire to escape from the complexities of human living. (Of course, the question immediately proposes itself, 'Who doesn't?') But his *final* attitude is not romantic; however great his longing for a perfect 'home' where he can find his 'rest' in beauty, he never deceives himself by excluding the painful. Much as the 'pure thrush word' means to him, he is ultimately in no need of Mr Eliot's (rather grim) warning of 'the deception of the thrush'; he values human consciousness:

> I could not be as the sun.
> Nor should I be content to be
> As little as the bird or as mighty as the sun.
> For the bird knows not of the sun,
> And the sun regards not the bird.
> But I am almost proud to love both bird and sun,
> Though scarce this Spring could my body leap four yards.
> *(Health)*

The emotion-shedding which in many writers is an

effect of the relief at the escape from complexity is absent from Thomas. In considering *Lights Out*, which is as direct an expression of feeling as anything in his poetry, we should disregard as far as we are able what it may seem to possess of prophecy; the poignancy doesn't need any adventitious stimulus:

> I have come to the borders of sleep,
> The unfathomable deep
> Forest where all must lose
> Their way, however straight
> Or winding, soon or late;
> They cannot choose.
>
> Many a road and track
> That, since the dawn's first crack,
> Up to the forest brink,
> Deceived the travellers,
> Suddenly now blurs,
> And in they sink.
>
> Here love ends,
> Despair, ambition ends;
> All pleasure and all trouble,
> Although most sweet or bitter,
> Here ends in sleep that is sweeter
> Than tasks most noble.
>
> There is not any book
> Or face of dearest look
> That I would not turn from now
> To go into the unknown
> I must enter, and leave, alone,
> I know not how.
>
> The tall forest towers;
> Its cloudy foliage lowers
> Ahead, shelf above shelf;
> Its silence I hear and obey
> That I may lose my way
> And myself.

Clearly the personal note is strong here, and the longing for sleep, that is, for the death of consciousness, is explicitly confessed; and the poignancy is the greater because the sleep is also death itself. But there is no self-absorbed gush of relief, and certain positives are expressed, simply but definitely: love, books, 'face of dearest look'. There is loss as well as gain in going out of life. The quietness of the tone—he is not falling upon the thorns of life and bleeding—and the control of the movement, together with the exactness of statement, make the total effect anything but one of facile indulgence. *Lights Out* is not as complex and meaningful as the best of Thomas; it tends to be on one note (perhaps fittingly, we may add, as a poem representing the feeling of just before sleep). But the simplicity is not that which comes of an adolescent attitude. Thomas, always aware of the tendency to desire to escape, knew that ultimately he could not:

> Recall
> Was vain: no more could the restless brook
> Ever turn back and climb the waterfall
> To the lake that rests and stirs not in its nook,
> As in the hollow of the collar-bone
> Under the mountain's head of rush and stone.
>
> (*Over the Hills*)

Here the rhythmical firmness, helping to convey the recognition of a strengthening 'moral' truth and the knowledge of an invigorating bleakness, carries a feeling the reverse of a desire to regress into a cosiness. Not that the 'mountain's head' itself is characteristically present in Thomas's poetry as a positive, a life-giving force. Mountains, sea, and sky are not normally offered by him in their capacity of giving power to men; we are made aware of them, in the main, as a kind of foil to the lives of smaller, moving creatures, including man.

EDWARD THOMAS

In the *Collected Poems*, *Lights Out* is immediately followed by *Cock-Crow*, and the contiguity serves to make the clearer the kind of self-awareness that was Thomas's. Here is *Cock-Crow*:

> Out of the wood of thoughts that grows by night
> To be cut down by the sharp axe of light,—
> Out of the night, two cocks together crow,
> Cleaving the darkness with a silver blow:
> And bright before my eyes twin trumpeters stand,
> Heralds of splendour, one at either hand,
> Each facing each as in a coat-of-arms:
> The milkers lace their boots up at the farms.

In this poem, with its firm movement, its vivid imagery, its grasp of external objects including those of the 'vision', we have moved away from the personal poignancy of *Lights Out*. Discussing *Cock-Crow* in *Scrutiny* (September, 1945), F. R. Leavis is concerned not only to demonstrate the subtlety of the imagery but to show that the total experience of the poem involves an *attitude towards* the imagery. The comment of his that is most relevant to the present discussion is this: 'The poet, aware as he wakes of the sound and the light together, has humoured himself in a half-waking dream-fantasy, which, when it has indulged itself to an unsustainable extreme of definiteness, suddenly has to yield to the recognition of reality.' There is a wakefulness, a realization of actualities of one kind or another, in all Thomas's poetry, from the delightful tender poems about the gifts he would make to Helen and his children—

> Her small hands I would not cumber
> With so many acres and their lumber,
> But leave her Steep and her own world
> And her spectacled self with hair uncurled,

> Wanting a thousand little things
> That time without contentment brings
> > (*What Shall I Give?*)

—to what is perhaps the bleakest poem of all, *Rain*:

> Rain, midnight rain, nothing but the wild rain
> On this bleak hut, and solitude, and me
> Remembering again that I shall die
> And neither hear the rain nor give it thanks
> For washing me cleaner than I have been
> Since I was born into this solitude. . . .

'Born into this solitude': writing about Thomas in the course of an article entitled 'A Note on Nostalgia' (*Determinations*, ed. F. R. Leavis), Mr D. W. Harding has this to say: 'In most of the poems there is no recognition of any underlying social cause for his feeling. Yet the quality of the melancholy so often suggests nostalgia that it is hard not to suppose that the unadmitted craving for an adequate social group lay behind his most characteristic moods.' Disagreement with Mr Harding on the point of 'nostalgia'—to me this word is quite inapt when used in reference to Thomas's poetry—does not at all invalidate the suggestion of an 'unadmitted craving for an adequate social group'. This suggestion may perhaps be linked profitably with what has been said in the present book about Thomas's 'vision' of nature and of civilization. Mr Harding is indicating an aspect of Thomas which we are likely to see as peculiarly 'modern'; that is, a sense of the painfulness of isolation, the isolation of the alert, conscious individual among the systematizing movements and tendencies of the 'modern world'. Thomas felt warmly towards a number of people, and he had the readiest response to anyone he met travelling the road, but he was not nourished by any feeling of human solidarity. He had no creed or set of beliefs to support—or appear to support

—him. His personal sympathies come into play in the face of what seems to be a complete lack of confidence in the human communal activities of the world. When he writes '. . . and the inn where all were kind, All were strangers', he is not being cynical by suggesting that further acquaintance will bring unkindness (though it might do so), and he is aware of men not only as 'strangers' but as 'kind', mankind, humankind; nevertheless, he does seem to be revealing that his love for the people he knew was not a steady source of strength to him.

There are times when Thomas feels that he would turn from the dearest human face; when he can speak of

> the dove
> That tempts me on to something sweeter than love;

when there is for him 'nothing but the wild rain'; when he can say that he has

> no love which this wild rain
> Has not dissolved except the love of death,
> If love it be for what is perfect and
> Cannot, the tempest tells me, disappoint.

But I cannot see that this sort of failure in human relationships (if, indeed, we consider it to be that), though it entailed some unhappiness for Thomas, did anything to diminish the strength of his individuality. His writing tends to be strong and sharp when his self-questioning and hence his isolation are deepest. That last line quoted above, for instance, with the sharp, distinct impact of 'cannot', so finely divided by the significant parenthesis from the final 'disappoint', and the consequent emphasis on that word even while it is at the same time 'negatived' by 'cannot', produces the same sort of positive strength out of an explicitly negative statement as we saw operating in that other final line of a poem:

> . . . I cannot bite the day to the core.

THE POETRY

The most extensive treatment, in a single poem, of the
theme of self-searching, is given in *The Other*. Describing
a quest for his deepest, his 'real' self, the poem begins thus:

> The forest ended. Glad I was
> To feel the light, and hear the hum
> Of bees, and smell the drying grass
> And the sweet mint, because I had come
> To an end of forest, and because
> Here was both road and inn, the sum
> Of what's not forest. But 'twas here
> They asked me if I did not pass
> Yesterday this way. 'Not you? Queer.'
> 'Who then? and slept here?' I felt fear.

This first verse suggests something of the interests and the
method of the poem: the inclusion in one experience of
'forest' and 'the sum Of what's not forest', the gladness, the
strange half-known man of 'yesterday', the 'fear'. He
pursues 'that other', trying the inns of 'a long gabled
high-street grey, Of courts and outskirts'. But he seeks in
vain, travelling 'An eager but a weary way'. (The poem
curiously recalls in one or two places *The Pilgrimage* of
George Herbert, whom Thomas had edited: in that poem
we have 'A long it was and weary way', and 'A wasted
place, but sometimes rich'. In some essentials, of course,
the poems are far apart.) The poet's goal is 'an unseen
moving' one, and he finds nothing but 'remedies For all
desire' and makes the discovery that he now wants to
desire something. He seems often to be close to 'him', but
cannot catch him. Leaving inns and people, he seeks in
solitude, with night falling and bringing a peace with it:

> I sought then in solitude.
> The wind had fallen with the night; as still
> The roads lay as the ploughland rude,
> Dark and naked, on the hill.

Had there been ever any feud
'Twixt earth and sky, a mighty will
Closed it: the crocketed dark trees,
A dark house, dark impossible
Cloud-towers, one star, one lamp, one peace
Held on an everlasting lease:

And all was earth's, or all was sky's;
No difference endured between
The two. A dog barked on a hidden rise;
A marshbird whistled high unseen;
The latest waking blackbird's cries
Perished upon the silence keen.
The last light filled a narrow firth
Among the clouds. I stood serene,
And with a quiet solemn mirth,
An old inhabitant of earth.

Once the name I gave to hours
Like this was melancholy, when
It was not happiness and powers
Coming like exiles home again,
And weaknesses quitting their bowers,
Smiled and enjoyed, far off from men,
Moments of everlastingness.
And fortunate my search was then
While what I sought, nevertheless,
That I was seeking, I did not guess.

That time was brief. . . .

He seeks again on the road and at the inn, and then
suddenly, 'amid a taproom's din', he hears his man asking
loudly for him, rebuking him and making him feel guilty
for thus everlastingly pursuing him and causing him (the
other) to feel as if he lives 'under a ban'. The pursuer says
nothing, and slips away:

And now I dare not follow after
Too close. I try to keep in sight,

Dreading his frown and worse his laughter.
I steal out of the wood to light;
I see the swift shoot from the rafter
By the inn door: ere I alight
I wait and hear the starlings wheeze
And nibble like ducks: I wait his flight.
He goes: I follow: no release
Until he ceases. Then I also shall cease.

The Other demands and richly repays the closest attention.
The search for a satisfying truth about himself, going on
against a background now of forest, quiet, solitude, darkness, now of noise and talk and company, is presented with
an incisiveness and a firmness of handling which at the
same time makes dramatic use of speech-rhythms. The
overlapping and mingling of one self with the other, making it impossible for the search to be successfully concluded in this life, is subtly conveyed throughout, even in
little seeming-ungrammatical ambiguities like 'What to do
When caught, I planned not', where, ostensibly seeking
the other, he is by the syntax made to refer to his own
capture; and when the other in the taproom complains
that he lives 'under a ban' because of the pursuer's
relentlessness, he is stating a condition which is precisely
central to the pursuer himself, and which we have been
made strongly to feel through all the vicissitudes of the
journey. The uncertainties involved in the seeker's intercourse at the inns are felt through the varying rhythms and
tones which are given to both narrative and comment, and
are, further, in significant contrast with that 'short-
lived) harmony when he was not a social being:

I stood serene,
And with a solemn quiet mirth,
An old inhabitant of earth.

EDWARD THOMAS

So vivid is the sensuous presentment that the journey is as
actual as it is symbolic, and a reality of the poet's spiritual
life is given through a situation which also, though 'in-
vented', has its own reality. The perplexing dichotomy of
being and knowing is perhaps the ultimate theme of the
poem. Thomas often touches upon this in his poems (and
elsewhere, as we have seen); in none of them does he make
such a dramatic and overt exploration of it as he does in
The Other.

'Forest' is one of the most frequent symbols in the
poetry, but when we attempt to fix its significance we
find not only that it varies subtly according to the context,
but also that our terms of explanation tend to sound heavy
and clumsy in comparison with the poet's touch. In rather
general terms we might say that 'forest' in Thomas's
poetry is the dark region of human experience which
cannot be illuminated by thought or reason, a pathless
region; it is the gulf of nothingness or eternity that waits
behind the temporal and the tangible; or it is simply
sleep, or death. The roads and inns that he loves are a
refuge from and a challenge to both the values of the
urban civilization he knew and the 'forest' of 'unknown
modes of being', of the region of the irrational, eternal
forces. Such a sense of the 'forest' can deepen, enrich,
refine consciousness, and it does so in Thomas. But it is
plain that the 'dark gods' are not a source of positive
power and *energy* to him; the characteristic effect of the
kind of knowledge he has of them is not to make him exult.
Occasionally we feel an exhilaration when he expresses
his apprehension of 'otherness':

> But the land is wild, and there's a spirit of wildness
> Much older, crying when the stone-curlew yodels
> His sea and mountain cry, high up in Spring.
>
> *(Up in the Wind)*

But this feeling is always momentary and is never wholly unmodified. Conversely, however, neither was the sense of a darkness, an immensity, existing behind the appearances and sounds of life, ever completely dominant. After the Christmas fair and market, going through the country-side he carries with him the thought, the image, the 'meaning' of the young gypsy and his mouth-organ:

> Not even the kneeling ox had eyes like the Romany.
> That night he peopled for me the hollow wooded land,
> More dark and wild than stormiest heavens, that I
>   searched and scanned
> Like a ghost new-arrived. The gradations of the dark
> Were like an underworld of death, but for the spark
> In the Gypsy boy's black eyes as he played and stamped
>   his tune,
> 'Over the hills and far away', and a crescent moon.
>
> (The Gypsy)

We could hardly be farther away from the feeling of rest-ing in nature; even the boy's eyes are black. But the spark is there, a fact; and while his tune, the name of it, suggests a drifting, an ever farther recession, we are told also that he 'stamped it': he is a human being with a physical existence on the earth; we note, too, that there is a moon, delicately new. The appreciation of life remains quick and sympathetic in the face of a philosophy or a metaphysic that is anything but 'optimistic'. In *Up in the Wind*, the barmaid at a lonely inn wishes that 'The road was nearer and the wind farther off', and complains that

> no one's moved the wood from off the hill
> There at the back, although it makes a noise
> When the wind blows; as if a train were running
> The other side, a train that never stops
> Or ends. And the linen crackles on the line
> Like a wood fire rising;

but she bends to her scrubbing with 'Not me: Not back to Kennington', and her long account of life at the inn, though by conscious intention an expression of uneasiness and loneliness, is alive with sensuous images and with sudden shifts of thought and feeling. The very persistence of the poet's interest in his 'fear' of 'forest' is in itself an active, positive trait, the antithesis of languor. And in the poetry there is an artist who can deal satisfactorily with the intimations.

The path had not been an easy one: he may have 'slipped into it naturally', as he told Hudson, but there had been almost a lifetime of preparation, and more than most poets he had to contend with his temperament and outlook while making his poetry out of them. Keen consciousness of an all-absorbing silence is not the best incitement that a poet can have to write down words confidently. The 'haunting sense of unreality', to use a phrase of Hawthorne's, had in some way and at least in some degree to be mastered. Consider, for instance, the extraordinarily interesting poem entitled *That Girl's Clear Eyes* (*Handel Street*):

> That girl's clear eyes utterly concealed all
> Except that there was something to reveal.
> And what did mine say in the interval?
> No more: no less. They are but as a seal
> Not to be broken till after I am dead;
> And then vainly. Every one of us
> This morning at our tasks left nothing said,
> In spite of many words. We were sealed thus,
> Like tombs. Nor until now could I admit
> That all I cared for was the pleasure and pain
> I tasted in the stony square sunlit,
> Or the dark cloisters, or shade of airy plane,
> While music blazed and children, line after line,
> Marched past, hiding the 'SEVENTEEN THIRTY-NINE'.

(At the end of Handel Street, in the parish of St Pancras, is the Foundlings' Hospital, founded by Thomas Coram in 1739. A statue of Coram, with that date on it, was standing in Thomas's day; it has since been removed. 'The stony square sunlit' is Brunswick Square. Many tomb-stones remain in the gardens thereabouts, and the plane trees are still there. The hospital band still plays the ranks of children through the gates next to which the statue stood.)

Even with the above information at hand, the poem is by no means 'easy to understand'. It may assist elucidation to point out that the first eight lines or so—the poem is a sonnet—are ostensibly relevant to the main title, and the last six to the sub-title (which is printed below the main title in the *Collected Poems*). The poem works round the idea of 'reality': the poet is asking himself what is most real, real for him. He states that the girl's eyes (the eyes, the very feature that should most vividly convey and express), say, or said, nothing except that they are concealing something. His own eyes are like the girl's: a significant reality is being concealed, and there can be no 'meeting' between the two human beings, saying so much and at the same time so little to each other. Even if death should reveal what this reality is (he does not say it will, for the document, envelope, that is sealed may have nothing in-side), the knowledge will be useless because there will then be no possibility of any 'meeting'. All words that are spoken say nothing in the end: the reality remains hidden. However, the poet now finds himself able or willing to 'admit' that it was not after all the possibility of 'meeting' another in a human relationship that most deeply engaged him, but the sensuous impressions, the square and the trees, sun and shade, children and music. But this ex-planation of the poem, suggesting that he is glad to escape from the difficult (human relationships) to the simple (the sensuous now), is not the whole truth; and it is, in fact, precisely in the little that is lacking that the essential meaning of the whole experience of the poem rests. The explanation given above is based altogether on the explicit statements of the poet; it doesn't take into account his language, the poet's language, his tone, mood, verbal structure. The structure looks simple enough: the first eight lines belong to the main title, *That Girl's Clear Eyes*, the last six to *Handel Street*. But in the very last phrase of the poem the poet comes back, seems just to manage to come back, to the theme of the first part, to the idea of concealment: these things that now attract him, the blazing music, the marching children, are themselves hiding a reality; in their attractiveness they (almost) blot out the memory of the pity and profound devotion of the founder of the hospital, a *Foundlings'* hospital. By that last phrase, 'hiding the SEVENTEEN THIRTY-NINE', we are taken a little distance from the present, which we are now likely to see as rather showy; we may wonder, too, whether that 'marched' is not, despite its splendour, half deprecatory, suggesting as it does the regimentation of children. There are other words and phrases that (we can now see) subtly modify his affirmation of a main interest in the surface, the immediacies: we note that he says 'pleasure *and* pain'; 'cared for' is not very positive, not enthusiastic; and the scene and the items that compose it themselves suggest conflicting feelings: the square is both stony and sunlit, there are dark, still cloisters and airy plane trees, and shadow from the trees. The 'pleasure and pain' is, of course, a reality for him; it is 'tasted', he wants to get the essence. But he brings us, and himself, back to the other reality also: the temptation to escape from the difficulties inherent in human 'meeting' has not been succumbed to after all. His victory seems to be only just a victory; but it is one. And it is one not because he can triumph in any very powerful way over circumstances, but because he is expressing a fine shade of consciousness, showing that he has won to a most delicate sincerity. Despite a certain weariness, a nonchalance threatening, he must continue to care. While we cannot say that *That Girl's Clear Eyes* (*Handel Street*) is characterized by power—the attitude and rhythms are hardly positive enough for that, the tone is rather low-pitched—it is, nevertheless, a remarkably fine poem, and one that readers of Thomas will want often to go back to.

What Will They Do? is another revealing poem with an urban setting: here, in the 'loud street', he feels he is 'naught' to the people whom he sees 'disappearing carelessly'; yet he wonders whether he is right in feeling so, and whether he himself doesn't 'nourish' something in them as they do in him. Thomas does not say what it is that may be nourished; it is something that 'has great value and no price'. But despite the lack of explanation, the final effect, which is reached with the aid of an image of rain, indispensable rain, nourishing the grass and flowers, is one of delicate self-searching. He doesn't want to believe that the rain is an indifferent, eternally neutral force; he would like to feel that it is itself conscious and that it is desirous of some sort of reciprocity from the grass and flowers. He half-wistfully thinks that the crowd ('rain') may be thirsting for 'a draught Which only in the blossom's chalice lies'; and we take the chalice, whether empty or containing nectar or water which the rain itself has brought, to be beauty of some kind, perhaps poetry, perhaps his own poetry. But at the end of the poem, with the turning back towards him of one who 'lightly laughed', he half-surrenders the dream, realizing that it involved a certain self-importance, and progresses to a further knowledge. The crowd, in one aspect, is still undifferentiated 'rain'; but a person can turn back out of it, it is also a crowd of living people. *What Will They Do?* is like *That Girl's Clear Eyes* in its delicately expressed balance and interplay between a feeling towards and a feeling away from human contacts. The impulse to share, and the something which thwarts it and impels towards aloofness: the predicament —and in much of the poem the 'I' is felt not as Edward Thomas only—and the sense of a man keenly conscious of his human individuality and at the same time of the ceaseless and 'inhuman' flow of life, are conveyed without strain in a poem which has a deal of 'direct statement' interwoven with the narrative-description and the imagery.

There are a few poems by Thomas that are of the 'direct statement' kind, lacking his characteristic expressive description. In poems like *No One So Much As You, Parting, To P. H. T.* (this last not added to the *Collected Poems* until 1949), he gives a sequence of explicit statements, using short lines to convey a certain sharpness, sometimes a grimness, of mood. The first and the last of those mentioned above are about love, one being to Helen and the other to his father. They have a similar terseness and an uncompromising tone, but the poem to his father, 'P. H. T.', is more simply a matter of bare assertion and is the more bitter and the less fine: beginning with

> I may come near loving you
> When you are dead
> And there is nothing to do
> And much to be said,

and ending with

> But not so long as you live
> Can I love you at all,

it is quietly hard and unforgiving. The poem to Helen is much less simple in its attitude: he recognizes and regrets the lack of a finally fulfilling communion with the loved one, and self-censure plays a large part in an analysis which seems intended to expose illusions and which yet has its tenderness. Here are three verses from the middle section of the poem:

> None ever was so fair
> As I thought you:
> Not a word can I bear
> Spoken against you.
>
> All that I ever did
> For you seemed coarse
> Compared with what I hid
> Nor put in force.
>
> My eyes scarce dare meet you
> Lest they should prove
> I but respond to you
> And do not love.

The only image in the poem occurs at the end, where he says he has often wondered whether it would have been better never to see her more

> Than linger here
>
> With only gratitude
> Instead of love—
> A pine in solitude
> Cradling a dove.

The image perfectly clinches his attitude: the tenderness implicit in it is played off against the seeming cruelty of the statement; the very last line softens, but does not annul, all that has gone before. In *Parting*, we have a pondering on the nature and character of the past, and on the nature of the pain of recalling it, and on his feelings now at

parting. The seeming paradox, but the actual fact, of the
past's ill becoming 'a kind of bliss' compared with the 'stir
and strain' of the present moment, and so, in spite of the
'bliss', mocking him the more, is beautifully led up to:

> Remembered joy and misery
> Bring joy to the joyous equally;
> Both sadden the sad. So memory made
>
> Parting to-day a double pain:
> First because it was parting; next
> Because the ill it ended vexed
> And mocked me from the Past again,
>
> Not as what had been remedied
> Had I gone on,—not that, oh no!
> But as itself no longer woe;
> Sighs, angry word and look and deed
>
> Being faded: rather a kind of bliss,
> For there spiritualized it lay
> In the perpetual yesterday
> That naught can stir or strain like this.

The best of the direct statement poems, with their keen
analysis of mood and condition which is at the same time
a conveying of the mood and condition, are excellent in
themselves as well as by their possessing an autobiographical interest of the more obvious kind. But they are
inevitably thinner than the best of the poems in which the
outer world is brought in as a force in the expression of
the poet's sensibility.

How that outer world does come in has been evident
from the quoted examples of the poetry. It is, of course,
almost entirely a rural world, and it is England; and no
one will dispute that Thomas (though also a townsman)
was a countryman in a way that gave him life. By accumulating from his poetry details about country people,

about farms, barns, orchards, trees, flowers, birds, the seasons, the counties, we can obtain for ourselves an England wonderfully seen and felt. He can beautifully and vividly evoke the Sunday quiet of an old farmhouse under the February sun, the darkness and antiquity of the Combe where the badger was dug out and killed, the feeling of the moment before work is resumed following the midday break on the haymaking field, the loneliness of a public house on the Downs; he can give a vivid impression of the man who sweeps leaves, of the watercress man, of barmaid, gypsy, huxter. We could easily say, 'This is England; this is Wiltshire, Hampshire, Surrey.' It *is* an England, deeply known. But Thomas does not care to give us more than a very little of the central and essential work of country people: the scenes are usually 'moments' that have a particular value for the poet; the country people tend to be casual workers, tramps, outcasts. When there is a shepherd in the poetry, it is not because of the interest or the value of his work. I labour this point perhaps—it was suggested in the previous comparison with Lawrence —in the endeavour to show that it was at bottom a certain lack of faith that prevented Thomas from dealing more fully in his poetry with rural *civilization*. I cannot see that this is a defect in him, though it obviously involves a limitation of range. I cannot see that the kind of negativeness that marks his outlook is to be deplored, the poetry being what it is. And it does not follow that a more positive attitude in the matter of rural sociology (even if we can imagine an Edward Thomas with such an attitude) would have produced better poetry.

Thomas would have listened as absorbedly as Richard Jefferies did to old Tibbald, the miller in *Round About a Great Estate*. But he would not primarily have handled in his writing (as Jefferies so superbly does) the old man's

speech, the details of his work, the associated economic
implications. He would have completely understood how
the decay of a tradition was embodied in Tibbald's situation, but he would not have made that decay the theme
of a poem. In *The Mill-Water*, the thought of the mill's
having once been 'a work-place and a home' is perhaps
the 'inspiration' of the poem, and the thought is most
poignantly felt; but he is not concerned so much with the
actual work and people of the now-finished mill as with
the 'idle foam', the sound of the water, especially at night,
and the silence. It is not the passing of a rural mode that
explicitly and primarily engages his interests and feelings,
but the passing of *all* human effort. Nevertheless, the
characteristic interweaving of fine perceptiveness and
delicate play of mind puts the poem at the other extreme
to a simple negativeness, a naïve gloom:

> Only the sound remains
> Of the old mill:
> Gone is the wheel;
> On the prone roof and walls the nettle reigns.
>
> Water that toils no more
> Dangles white locks
> And, falling, mocks
> The music of the mill-wheel's busy roar.
>
> Pretty to see, by day
> Its sound is naught
> Compared with thought
> And talk and noise of labour and of play.
>
> Night makes the difference.
> In calm moonlight,
> Gloom infinite,
> The sound comes surging in upon the sense:

Solitude, company,—
When it is night,—
Grief or delight
By it must haunted or concluded be.

Often the silentness
Has but this one
Companion;
Wherever one creeps in the other is:

Sometimes a thought is drowned
By it, sometimes
Out of it climbs;
All thoughts begin or end upon this sound,

Only the idle foam
Of water falling
Changelessly calling,
Where once men had a work-place and a home.

Thomas, then, perceives the life and things of rural
England with an imaginative sympathy which, while he
does not relate them to any powerful controlling humane
conception, makes them a source of spiritual-sensuous
strength to him, and so through his art to us. When he
contemplates a barn he is acutely aware of what it is, for
him, now, as it stands before him; and while, in lines like

No abbey or castle looks so old
As this that Job Knight built in '54,

he intimates (so quietly) his awareness of the continuity
and age of tradition, and gives us a real country name, Job
Knight, that suggests both Bible and feudalism, it is not
that kind of interest that he develops most. His interest is
not like John Durbeyfield's interest in the tombs of the
d'Urbervilles. He sees the barn primarily as a place of
habitation, and a habitation *shared* by the diverse creatures
which are carrying on a life older than man's abbeys and

castles. There are rats, for the barn was 'Built to keep corn for rats and men'; there are 'fowls on the roof, pigs on the floor', the roof where 'only fowls have foothold enough', and where 'What thatch survives is dung for the grass, The best grass on the farm'; starlings used to nest in the thatch, the starlings that

> used to sit there with bubbling throats
> Making a spiky beard as they chattered
> And whistled and kissed, with heads in air,

but the roof is now too dilapidated even for them, and 'It's the turn of lesser things'. The kind of quick observation (using the word in both its normal senses) in evidence here, springs from a beautifully spontaneous sympathy. What he says about the life of the creatures springs out of what he sees *now* in front of him. In another poem, when he has stacked up 'fifty faggots That once were underwood of hazel and ash In Jenny Pinks's Copse', he remarks that

> Next Spring
> A blackbird or a robin will nest there,
> Accustomed to them, thinking they will remain
> Whatever is for ever to a bird:
> This Spring it is too late; the swift has come.
>
> *(Fifty Faggots)*

The kind of thinking that is contained here, a reflecting that links present and past and future, spontaneously associating what is with what has been and what will be, represents one kind of imagination. It rises out of a certainty of knowledge and a gladness in the knowledge, out of a profound sincerity of interest, profound in the sense that it was rooted and habitual in Thomas's character. He doesn't parade or proclaim this gift: he offers with an easy quiet naturalness his records of the kind of sympathy which enriched and helped to sustain him.

It may have become clear from the quoted poems and passages that the diction is as free from poeticalities as the movement in its communication of the play of feeling and of the developing thought is free from rigidity. There are very few clichés in Thomas's poetry; and though he has his 'favourite' common words—sweet, solitary, happy, once, shade, strange, vainly, hidden—these are almost invariably *used* as an essential element in the whole poem, modified by and modifying other elements, and not exploited for their stock emotional value; the attitudes lying behind their use are fresh. In *Lights Out*, the response invited by the seeming commonplace 'face of dearest look' is sharply modified by the immediately following 'That I would not turn from now'. Similarly the 'sweeter than love' that occurs near the beginning of *The Glory*,

> . . . and the dove
> That tempts me on to something sweeter than love,

seems to invite a conventional warmth of response, but the whole line, far from representing a simple surrender to a cliché value, will be seen in its context to state coolly a truth for the poet, setting up a balance between warmth towards the object and a direct unemotional statement. When we read of 'Old Jack Noman . . . With a cowslip bunch in his button-hole And one in his cap', that 'He was welcome as the nightingale' (the poem is called *May the Twenty-third*), the reality of the mood and scene has been so established that what the seemingly trite simile says is felt to be simply true: Old Jack was as welcome to this poet as that transcendently beautiful song. And his nightingales, despite the note of longing in much of the poetry, do not belong with the attitude of 'The wrong of unshapely things is a wrong too great to be told'. He speaks, in *Women He Liked*, of a

> track that had never had a name
> For all its thicket and the nightingales
> That should have earned it:

there is no poeticality about that 'earned'. His thrushes *pack* their unwilling *hoard* of song into that last hour of the wintry March day. An April morning is '*stirring* and sweet And warm'. The 'pink sham flowers' of a gypsy are no bar to her 'grace' (nor, incidentally, are they seized upon as an occasion for smart comment or moralizing). When an odd-job country worker is met by Thomas on the road, the 'brolly' that he carries is not seen as fantastic or amusing or picturesque; it is simply accepted along with the flag-basket and the old coat as part of this old country-man's character and life. Ultimately it is Thomas's lack of condescension, his readiness to respond, his openness to impressions, that give his language a certain breadth and diversity and keep it from the falsities and limitations imposed by ready-made notions of the 'poetical'.

That the words of his poetry should be notably those of everyday speech is perhaps what we should expect from one who had the feeling at once generous and quietly chastening, and never hardening into a moralistic principle, of a common destiny for men and creatures:

> A grey flycatcher silent on a fence
> And I sat as if we had been there since
> The horseman and the horse lying beneath
> The fir-tree-covered barrow on the heath,
> The horseman and the horse with silver shoes,
> Galloped the downs last.   (*The Brook*)

The moment conveys a sense of affinity with the living bird and with the dead horseman and horse, and because the different objects are given an equal value in the poet's mind and feelings and in his words, there is an effect of sure, quiet balance. This balance is a feature of the

poetry as a whole. In *The Brook* itself there is himself,
grown up, and the child; she is paddling and active, he is
seated, receiving, observant; there is the butterfly that
alights (softly) on the (hard) rounded stone that the cart-
horse often kicks against; he and the butterfly are enjoy-
ing sun and earth; there is movement and 'eternity':

> The waters running frizzled over gravel,
> That never vanish and for ever travel;

there is himself silent, and the bird silent; the cart-horse
and the galloping horse; the horse galloping and the
horse at rest; present and past, life and death. What we
have is not the 'violent yoking together of heterogeneous
ideas', but a situation where a variety of perceptions and
feelings and thoughts are *quietly* brought together to form
a balanced whole. Here is the complete poem:

> Seated once by a brook, watching a child
> Chiefly that paddled, I was thus beguiled.
> Mellow the blackbird sang and sharp the thrush
> Not far off in the oak and hazel brush,
> Unseen. There was a scent like honeycomb
> From mugwort dull. And down upon the dome
> Of the stone the cart-horse kicks against so oft
> A butterfly alighted. From aloft
> He took the heat of the sun, and from below.
> On the hot stone he perched contented so,
> As if never a cart would pass again
> That way; as if I were the last of men
> And he the first of insects to have earth
> And sun together and to know their worth.
> I was divided between him and the gleam,
> The motion, and the voices, of the stream,
> The waters running frizzled over gravel,
> That never vanish and for ever travel.
> A grey flycatcher silent on a fence
> And I sat as if we had been there since

The horseman and the horse lying beneath
The fir-tree-covered barrow on the heath,
The horseman and the horse with silver shoes,
Galloped the downs last. All that I could lose
I lost. And then the child's voice raised the dead.
'No one's been here before' was what she said
And what I felt, yet never should have found
A word for, while I gathered sight and sound.

The tangible and the intangible, the clear and the
misty, the sensuous and the symbolic, the near and the
far, the common and the rare, light and shade, movement
and stillness, sound and silence, earth and sky, action and
thought: these are some of the more obvious dualities that
occur again and again in Thomas's poetry. They are, of
course, 'obvious' only when abstracted from the living
moments which the poetry provides. Nor is it upon their
presence alone that the balance which we have been considering depends. Even the smaller poems often show that
the balance is one of manner and tone, manner and tone
felt through the technique. *A Cat* is one of Thomas's
simpler poems:

> She had a name among the children;
> But no one loved though someone owned
> Her, locked her out of doors at bedtime
> And had her kittens duly drowned.
>
> In Spring, nevertheless, this cat
> Ate blackbirds, thrushes, nightingales,
> And birds of bright voice and plume and flight,
> As well as scraps from neighbours' pails.
>
> I loathed and hated her for this;
> One speckle on a thrush's breast
> Was worth a thousand such; and yet
> She lived long, till God gave her rest.

The sympathy evoked by the account of the unkind treatment of the animal—we note the stressed 'her', we are not dealing with an animal as 'it'—is seemingly banished by the facts of the second verse: notwithstanding the harsh treatment the cat goes on with her life, and goes on without 'sentimentality', the birds being to her an item of food like the scraps from the pails. So she is 'loathed and hated': the fierce feeling in the commonplace words is the feeling that he would have when he actually came upon a bird-killing, when he saw, the horror is suggested, a detached feather with a speckle upon it. But after his expression, in his hatred, of his opinion of the cat's 'worth' in comparison with the thrush, comes the recognition of the cat's life, her place in the scheme of things, her lifelong struggle for survival: that 'and yet' in the last line but one not only leads into the statement of the final line, but also throws a doubt back, as we read, over the preceding 'Was worth a million such'. *A Cat* is a minor poem in Thomas's *œuvre*, but the attitude it presents, an attitude which involves acceptance of a distressing fact in nature, a placing of the fact within a larger view but without evading the fact's unpleasantness, is not so common either in life or in literature that we should pass it without notice. What was referred to above as 'an effect of sure, quiet balance' indicates a mastery in at least some fields of experience, and also a corresponsive command of words.

Another help towards a balanced attitude is humour, and Thomas had thought too seriously about life not to have developed subtle shades of it. We have, in fact, already seen that humour is to be met with in his writings from the start. But the last thing that the poetry would suggest is that Edward Thomas was 'fundamentally a humorist' (Thomas Seccombe could scarcely have held this opinion if he had been acquainted with the poetry). I do not think there is a single poem by Thomas—and

I am not forgetting *Lob*—that we should characterize primarily as humorous. Where humour comes in, and it comes in often, its usual effect is to widen and subtilize the tone and so make us feel the more fully the reality and truth of the whole that the poem presents; when we smile at a felicity it is often with the inward comment, 'Yes, that's right'. The humour is not of the type that turns us off from central considerations; it is never an invitation to evasion, it doesn't shelter but widens and confirms. In *Wind and Mist*, when the young man (Thomas himself) who had lived in a house on the top of a lonely hill, comes to tell his interlocutor about the wind, his conversational and half-serious tone, both polite and dry, makes him the more real and his feelings about the wind the more 'serious':

> . . . I had forgot the wind.
> Pray do not let me get on to the wind.
> You would not understand about the wind.
> It is my subject, and compared with me
> Those who have always lived on the firm ground
> Are quite unreal in this matter of the wind.

The truth for the poet, for this poet in particular, that those last three lines express, is not at all diminished by the half-mocking half-confident tone and the exaggerated emphasis on 'wind'. It is humour, too, that gives the quietly jolting effect at the end of *There's Nothing Like the Sun*, where, after being concerned to record a beautiful gratitude, through some twenty lines, for the sun that is kind to 'Stones and men and beasts and birds and flies', he gives us this final line:

> There's nothing like the sun till we are dead.

These 'humorous' effects cannot be fully appreciated, especially when they depend on anti-climax, except in the context of the complete poem. *May the Twenty-third* has forty lines or so of light-hearted description of a fine day and of Old Jack with his cresses and cowslips, and there is fresh and lively dialogue; but here are the concluding lines of the poem:

> Of the dust in my face, too, I was glad.
> Spring could do nothing to make me sad.
> Bluebells hid all the ruts in the copse,
> The elm seeds lay in the road like hops,
> That fine day, May the twenty-third,
> The day Jack Noman disappeared.

Despite the hints (how delicately conveyed) that we may gather from 'dust', 'sad', 'ruts' (the past, antiquity, is there though he says the bluebells of the moment hide it), and the elms seeding (so early in the year), despite these reminders of time, that last line comes with a suddenness, felt the more because it is rhythmically quite in tune with all that goes before, that is at least in part humorous in effect. The poet leads us on, and lets us down into nothing. The last line casts a certain hue—of what depth it seems impossible to determine—over the preceding liveliness; up till then the humour had seemed to reside in the walk and talk and appearance of Old Jack.

When Thomas writes about country people, his humour is never condescending. They say odd things, but they are likely to be terse and brisk, as when the old Jack-of-all-trades in *Man and Dog* tells the stranger about his life:

> He fell once from a poplar tall as these:
> The Flying Man they called him in hospital.
> 'If I flew now, to another world I'd fall.'

In *Lovers*, there is an interchange of half-shocked and half-excited comment between George and Jack as they see the lovers come out of the wood; their final remark is, 'What a thing it is, this picking may!' Similar to this quick gathering of odd but often striking turns of language is the 'imaginative' eye's perceiving or creating an odd aspect in common things. The slightly disturbing and so enlivening way of seeing, whereby the birds in the depth of the hollow wood are 'Fish that laugh and shriek', is not arbitrary and simply grotesque; it is 'truthful', too, and it is touched with humour. And in *The New Year*, what at first may seem to be far-fetched images and figures of speech, turn out, when we consider them carefully, to be strangely truthful:

> He was the one man I met up in the woods
> That stormy New Year's morning; and at first sight,
> Fifty yards off, I could not tell how much
> Of the strange tripod was a man. His body
> Bowed horizontal, was supported equally
> By legs at one end, by a rake at the other:
> Thus he rested, far less like a man than
> His wheel-barrow in profile was like a pig.

Even the wheel-barrow-pig comparison will be found amusingly right when we test it by experience. Wholly characteristic, in ways that do not need any comment here, is the transition, at this point of the poem, to

> But when I saw it was an old man bent,
> At the same moment came into my mind
> The games at which boys bend thus, *High-cocolorum*,
> Or *Fly-the-garter*, and *Leap-frog*.

Lob would certainly be considered by most readers of Thomas to be among the most 'joyous' of his poems: we feel the pleasure the poet has in his handling of a quantity of diverse material, and the poem has its own kind of opulence. But though the verbal dexterity and the intimate tone beautifully serve a love of places, folk-lore, flowers and flower-names, and so on, the poem has moments like this:

THE POETRY

> . . . And, Hob being then his name,
> He kept the hog that thought the butcher came
> To bring his breakfast. 'You thought wrong', said Hob.
> When there were kings in Kent this very Lob . . .

and this:

> And though he never could spare time for school
> To unteach what the fox so well expressed,
> On biting the cock's head off,—Quietness is best,—

and this:

> You see those bits
> Of mounds—that's where they opened up the barrows
> Sixty years since, while I was scaring sparrows.
> They thought as there was something to find there,
> But couldn't find it, by digging, anywhere:

moments where the humour of the smile is slightly though surely tinted with something else. So that although it abounds with exquisite unforced humour, *Lob* is by no means unequivocally humorous. The humour is exquisite precisely because the flow of enjoyed instances and details is controlled by the sharp thoughtful mind, and controlled without expense to the friendly, intimate tone. *Lob* is a delightful poem; its humour is in no way 'delicious'.

The absence of 'delicious' appeal is one of the things that distinguish Thomas's poetry from both Victorian romantic poetry and the poetry of many of his contemporaries, and it is probably this absence that has been the main cause of the comparative neglect and the incomplete understanding, and sometimes the complete misunderstanding, of his poetry. To readers expecting or demanding that they should find in poetry the swoon or rush into emotion, or predominantly a melodious-pictorial charm, or an immediately understood commerce with nature, or versified sentiments, or an escape into an overt dream-world of one kind or another, to these readers in the 'romantic tradition' Thomas's poetry either appeared to be 'puzzling' or was assimilable into that tradition. The themes and feelings of his poetry being what they were, it was almost inevitable that a superficial reading should result in that last fate being his. And yet even in his 'nature' and his 'melancholy' and his 'love' he stands apart from the Victorian manifestations of those subjects. If we put a poem by Arnold, acknowledged to be one of the least gross and one of the most modern of the Victorians, by the side of a Thomas poem, we are aware of a significant difference. If we look at *Requiescat* or the autumn-evening description from *Rugby Chapel*, and then at *Melancholy*—'The rain and wind, the rain and wind, raved endlessly'—we see in the Thomas not only a more exquisite particularity in the presentment of the immediate scene, the particularity having an essential function in the presentment of a greater complexity and rareness of mood, but also the presence of cool, distinct statement *with* the evocative, and relished, verbal beauty:

> . . . Yet naught did my despair
> But sweeten the strange sweetness, while through the
>   wild air
> All day long I heard a distant cuckoo calling
> And, soft as dulcimers, sounds of near water falling,
> And, softer, and remote as if in history,
> Rumours of what had touched my friends, my foes, or me.

Thomas's poetry, lacking though it is in powerfully suggestive and far-reaching imagery, shows poetic thought functioning in a way that is fundamentally alien to nineteenth-century fashion.

It was as a heartening contrast to the most offending aspects of nineteenth-century poetry that Thomas delighted in the work of Robert Frost. 'These poems are revolutionary because they lack the exaggeration of rhetoric', was one of his comments when reviewing *North of Boston* in 1914 (quoted by Eleanor Farjeon in an article about Frost and Thomas in *The London Magazine*, May, 1954). Usually, when he wrote about Frost, he either stated or implied that contemporary poetry could profit by 'absolute fidelity to the postures which the voice assumes in the most expressive intimate speech', indicating, however (as in the letter to Bottomley previously quoted from), that these tones and postures are not necessarily to be conveyed in the 'very words and structures of common speech'. It is plain that the concern to support Frost was the more eager because Thomas was at the same time working out ideas that mattered to himself.

The encouragement given by Frost to Thomas was not only direct and overt but was through example also. This does not mean that there are not essential differences between Frost's poetry and Thomas's, or that Thomas was not justified when defending his originality in a letter to Hudson: 'I would very much rather know that you like or don't wholly like a thing than that somebody else thinks it a pity I ever read Frost,' etc. I should say that the direction in which the debt mostly lay was in the affection and admiration he felt for Frost on account of his themes and his way of presenting them; the manner showed a way of feeling and thinking which was extremely sympathetic to Thomas. Here was a poet who really did know a lot about out-of-doors life, who didn't patronize country people, who was indifferent to social differentiation, who farmed and also strolled and talked and enjoyed picking berries from a hedge. In Frost, too, there are lonely houses, dark trees, tramps and miscellaneous workers, paths, the edge of the forest, the wind in the dark, sounds of flowing water. Thomas did not, of course, take these over from Frost; they were all, as we have seen, significant interests in his prose from the start. But it must have delighted him to find such things in the American poet. He may even have derived from Frost a kind of sanction for that which he himself wished to write. There were, moreover, explicit sentiments and ideas in Frost's work to which he must have keenly responded:

> 'It all depends on what you mean by home.'
> '. . . I should have called it
> Something you somehow haven't to deserve';

and

> Earth's the right place for love;

and

> You make a little foursquare block of air,
> Quiet and light and warm, in spite of all
> The illimitable dark and cold and storm.

And occasionally a line in Thomas may seem to be an echo of a line in Frost, as when

> You would not understand about the wind

may recall to some readers

> You don't know what I mean about the flowers.

But despite the number of easily seen resemblances, there can be no question of 'imitation'. Perhaps Thomas would have written no poetry, his death coming when it did, if he had not known Frost; it seems certain he would have written less. But he is an original poet. Like most good poets, he is helped by what in others he has admired and loved (and we must not forget that he had known much poetry before he met with Frost's), but the technique achieved—both warrant and expression of lived experience—is his own. Robert Frost is an original poet too, with his own excellences. As I see it, the poetry of the practised poet was just the right sort of *immediate* stimulus for the 'beginner' who was to go some distance beyond it by virtue of possessing what it is not invidious to call a finer vision and a correspondingly finer and more concentrated use of language.

There are, of course, among Thomas's poems some which do not fully show his unique qualities, slight poems in which he is not fully engaged; and there are poems which are not wholly successful. Occasionally his use of words like 'dearest' and 'fairest' may be felt to have no great depth or very strong pressure behind it; and he sometimes allows himself to be satisfied (because of his dislike of rhetoric) with a rhythm that has little impulse in it, a movement and tone that are too conversational. But there are extraordinarily few places where we can point to perfunctory rhythms or to actual faults in tone, and even in the very short and the less ambitious poems, and in those parts where we may feel a lack of 'bite', a careful reading will almost always reveal some characteristic attitude and touch. Thomas's poetry is notable for the consistency with which it displays his particular excellences.

If we say it is minor poetry, it is chiefly because his range is limited; the preoccupation is personal, he is concerned with his own condition and moods. But though the poetry does not take in much of the outward circumstance of the age he lived in, the mind and spirit in and behind it is modern in its delicately exploring tendency, its refusal to accept any of the old sanctions and forms simply because they are sanctions and forms, its chastening but not overwhelming apprehension of time and eternity, its sense of isolation. Possibly we might postulate a more positive attitude to experience as essential to a writer if he is to be reckoned 'major', though I should say that those by whom Thomas might be considered unduly negative would turn out to be, in the main, those who believe they find or hope to find strength and salvation in a creed or programme of one sort or another, religious, social, economic, political. In any case, our final emphasis must fall not on stature but on the sensitive life. He made poems out of what would be called slight events and unimposing situations, poems that are fresh and beautiful on the surface and rich underneath. He had the eye to see and the voice to tell that bare elm-tops are 'delicate as flower of grass'; and the whole body of his poetry is there to show that when he writes

> As well as any bloom upon a flower
> I like the dust on the nettles, never lost
> Except to prove the sweetness of a shower,

the affirmation that he is making, with its suggestion of a depth which both modifies and enhances the surface meaning, is simply true. A ruined cottage told him a tale hardly less deep and moving than Margaret's told to Wordsworth; and I do not know of any poet who could say better than he what the wind can mean when it is heard suddenly for the first time in the new house. The voice with which he spoke in his poetry has the rare quality of being at once subtle and unassuming. And both from its words and its tone we know that he was sensitively and generously alive. His feeling or his knowledge of a silent emptiness on the other side of the hill did not impede his wonderfully quick sympathy with the things on this side: he is at the opposite pole to the mockery and bitterness that frustration often gives rise to. Out of the gulf 'where nothing is But what is not' he was glad to come into the sensuous present,

> To feel the light, and hear the hum
> Of bees, and smell the drying grass
> And the sweet mint;

but he never evaded the gulf, in his poetry he built no castles: for him the earth was 'lovelier Than any mysteries'. On the edge of the forest there is always a thrush that twiddles his song; but the forest remains. Perhaps it would have receded a little if he had lived longer; he might have come to express more feelings, and in a larger context, than he did in fact express; it is even possible that certain antipathies and frustrations might have been liberated to combine with the sympathies and form a more powerful poetry. But our concern is with the poems we have, and even here the achievement, the achieved technique in face of the recognition so finely voiced at the end of *The Glory*—

> How dreary-swift, with naught to travel to,
> Is Time? I cannot bite the day to the core

—does represent a triumph over his self-distrust and his suffering. Not the least of the impressions that we gather from Edward Thomas's poetry is one of strength, the strength of a self-reliant seeker, the strength of individuality.

Appendix

THERE are some thirty books of prose by Edward
Thomas, and they may helpfully be given a certain
grouping. *Horae Solitariae* (1902), *The Rose Acre Papers*
(1904, and an enlarged version in 1910), *Rest and Unrest*
(1910), *Light and Twilight* (1911), *Cloud Castle* (1922), and
The Last Sheaf (1928) are books of essays with miscellaneous subjects. The more purely nature and country books
may form another group: *The Woodland Life* (1897), *The
Heart of England* (1906), *The South Country* (1909), *The
Country* (1913), *The Icknield Way* (1913), *In Pursuit of
Spring* (1914); also included here may be *The Happy-Go-
Lucky Morgans* (1913) and *Beautiful Wales* (1905). *Oxford*
(1903), *Windsor Castle* (1910), and *The Isle of Wight* (1911)
are topographical books. The literary criticism group,
which of course includes biographical material, is the
largest: *Richard Jefferies* (1909), *Feminine Influence on the
Poets* (1910; Chapter VIII was published separately in
1911 as *The Tenth Muse*), *Maurice Maeterlinck* (1911),
Algernon Charles Swinburne (1912), *George Borrow* (1912),
Lafcadio Hearn (1912), *Walter Pater* (1913), *Keats* (1916),
and *A Literary Pilgrim in England* (1917). *The Life of the
Duke of Marlborough* appeared in 1915. Other books were
Celtic Stories (1911), *Norse Tales* (1912), *Four and Twenty
Blackbirds* (1915). In 1938 *The Childhood of Edward Thomas*
was published; it seems to have been written mostly in
1913.

A good deal of miscellaneous reviewing by Thomas
appeared in *The Daily Chronicle*, *The English Review*,

APPENDIX

Poetry and Drama, etc., and he wrote Introductions for an edition of John Dyer's Poems (1903), and for Dent's Everyman volumes of Borrow's *Bible in Spain* (1906) and *Gipsies of Spain* (1914), of George Herbert's *Poems* (1908), *Marlowe* (1909), Isaac Taylor's *Words and Places* (1911), and *Rural Rides* (1912). He also compiled two anthologies, each with a short introduction by himself: *The Pocket Book of Poems and Songs for the Open Air* (1907) and *This England* (1915); and he edited *The Pocket George Borrow*.

Further details will be found in R. P. Eckert's Bibliography, which must be virtually complete.

NOTE TO THE APPENDIX: 1973

Three books which have been published since 1956 testify to the renewal of interest in Edward Thomas. These are: *Edward Thomas: The Last Four Years*, Book One of the Memoirs of Eleanor Farjeon (Oxford University Press 1958); *Letters from Edward Thomas to Gordon Bottomley*, edited by R. George Thomas (Oxford University Press 1968); and *Edward Thomas, a Critical Biography 1878-1917* by William Cooke (Faber & Faber 1970).

Index

INDEX

INDEX

INDEX

254

INDEX

255

INDEX